KINSHIP:
It's All Relative

Portrait of the author by Patricia Hill Burnett

KINSHIP

It's All Relative

by

Jackie Smith Arnold

Second Edition

Enlarged with a New Chapter on Same-Sex Marriage

First Edition, 1990
Second Edition, 1994
Second Edition enlarged with a new chapter on same-sex marriage,
2012

Published by Genealogical Publishing Co., Inc.
3600 Clipper Mill Road, Suite 260
Baltimore, Maryland 21211
Library of Congress Catalogue Card Number 2012936215
International Standard Book Number 978-0-8063-1953-7
Made in the United States of America

Dedication

To my three sons, David Michael Batts,
Charles Howard Batts, and Thomas Alan Batts

In Memory of Charles Howard Batts

Acknowledgments

Thank you to Colin Partlin, legal researcher, for his contribution of time and energy in reviewing the chapter on same-sex marriage. Special thanks to Tom Batts and David Batts for their encouragement, and to Amanda Batts for her insight concerning the education of young children. And, last but not least, gratitude to my multitude of Smith cousins for their sense of family, especially Billy and Marisha Hall and George Earl Smith.

As always I am grateful to Michael Tepper, Eileen Perkins, and Joe Garonzik of Genealogical Publishing Company for their professional guidance.

Contents

Introduction   ix

1 • Kinship   1
Why does kinship matter? • How the family got
started • Enter the patriarchy

2 • Marriage   7
Marriage • Divorce • Live-ins

3 • Kinship Groups   25
Belonging to a family • Types of family • Ascents and descents
• Three families at once

4 • Our Three Families   31
Family of orientation • Family of procreation • Family
of affinity

5 • Family   49
Family defined • Family law • Children • Adoption •
Adoption annulments • Responsibilities to other
relatives • Grandparents' rights • Grandparents
resource test • Miscellaneous • Vital statistics

6 • Names   71
Surnames of married women • Surnames of
children • First names • Name changes

7 • Wills   77

8 • Kinship and Your Health   **85**
Your genetic inheritance • AI, in vitro, and surrogacy •
Medical charts

Medical Charts   **93**
Children • Siblings • Self and spouse • Parents •
Grandparents • Great-grandparents

9 • Tracing Your Family Tree   **97**
Family history • Immediate sources • More distant
sources • Why research?

10 • Kinship and the Future   **103**
Families in the future • Kinship, who needs it?

Epilogue   **107**

Bibliography and Reference List   **111**

Glossary   **113**

Index   **121**

Kinship Update: Same-Sex Marriage   **125**

Introduction

"Where shall I begin, please Your Majesty?" he asked. "Begin at the beginning," the King said, gravely...

Lewis Carroll, Alice In Wonderland

Robert Frost said, "Home is the place; when you go there, they have to take you in." But home may have many different meanings. To some people it may mean a particular house or town, while to others, home may be a spiritual ideal carried from place to place as if it were an ethereal appendage. One thing is for certain—home, whether concrete or abstract, is always inhabited by relatives; our kin, blood of our blood.

Relatives are people we get stuck with at birth, for better or worse; chapels of pride or citadels of shame, or a combination of both. They must be invited to family reunions and notified of funerals. Relatives share our ancestors and peek at us through the leaves of the family tree. They are near and far, shirt-tail and kissin' kin, and all degrees in between.

Why is blood relationship of great interest to some people, while others couldn't care less? Have you ever wondered why various cousins are designated "removed" and others are not? And what does removed mean, anyway? Is your legal next-of-kin the same as your closest biological relative?

Why do civil incest laws prohibit you from marrying certain relatives? In the United States, it's illegal for first cousins to marry in some states but acceptable in others. Do laws pander to the whims of powerful personalities, such as the Roman emperor Claudius, who forced the senate to repeal its ban against uncle/niece marriages so he could marry Agrippina, whose son Nero eventually fiddled while Rome burned? Or Henry VIII, who sought a way to remove Catherine of Aragon and marry Anne Boleyn. Since divorce was out of the question, Henry pointed to a passage in the Bible, "If a man shall take his brother's wife it is an unclean thing. ..." Now, that little passage from Leviticus hadn't bothered anyone when the young couple had originally married. But Henry used it to have the union declared incestuous, and his marriage to Catherine was subsequently annulled.

The diversity of kinship laws in the United States can be traced via tangled roots running back to the 21st century B.C. when the Sumerians became the first people to record their laws. A couple of centuries later, Hammurabi developed his 282 codes of conduct, of which 68 dealt specifically with disputes between relatives.

However, the rules that have most greatly affected Western familial society are the commandments inscribed on the stone tablets Moses brought down from the mount around 1200 B.C.—"Thou shalt honor thy father and thy mother..."; "Thou shalt not covet thy neighbor's wife..."; "Thou shall not commit adultery   "

Napoleon I reformed the legal system of France by borrowing many of the principles and practices of the Greeks and Romans who had preceded him. When French-settled Louisiana became a state in 1812, it retained the Napoleonic Code of 1804 as the basis of its civil laws; some of those laws are still in use today and govern many familial situations.

Basic English common law came to the American colonies with the earliest English settlers. Common law is made up of case law, or judge-made law; it is constantly evolving and relies heavily on previous court decisions (precedent). Alongside the judge-made law, we apply statutory law, which is made up of acts adopted by state legislatures and the United States Congress.

However, except for certain basic rules, the law generally has ignored actions kept within kinship circles. Until fairly recently, a man's home was truly his castle. The Roman **paterfamilias** (head of the household) exercised total control over his wife, his children, their spouses and offspring, and all his slaves or servants. He had the right to banish disobedient adults, sell unwanted children, or kill infants he decided were too frail to lead productive, healthy lives.

In the United States, our laws now determine whom one may marry, and how one must treat one's spouse and children. Laws settle disputes within the family and between differing family units. Interfamily blood feuds are no longer tolerated, but some states have wrongful death statutes which permit a surviving relative to sue someone who has wrongfully killed a parent, spouse, or child. The courts generally consider the victim's professional status and work record in order to determine a punitive payment.

American courts are beginning to address questions concerning children born of modern technology (surrogacy, in vitro fertilization, or artificial insemination) and whether such children have legal rights to know their ancestors and to socialize with their biological kin.

And, who might that kin be?

Let's open the door of kinship and meet those relatives foisted upon us because of birth and by the laws of the land. Like a crazy quilt inherited from a great-great-grandmother, there is much to delight and to tease. But look beyond the neat stitching and the rainbow colors, and you'll see more than first meets the eye.

* * *

Laws and customs, like the proverbial river, change constantly. A small book can't be expected to give comprehensive advice, nor does it attempt to. Your specific questions can best be answered by consulting appropriate magistrates, agencies, or attorneys.

1 • Kinship

... One touch of nature makes the whole world kin....
Shakespeare

Why does kinship matter?

Kinship, degrees, removed! Are you confused, perplexed, or bored when it comes to determining how close your relatives are? And if it's all that confusing, forget it—who cares?

Believe it or not, some people are more interested in your **pedigree** (a register recording lines of ancestors) than in your astrological birth sign. The Daughters of the American Revolution demand a proper pedigree. Genealogical societies not only need kinship, they swear by it.

And there are compelling reasons to be interested in kinship. Personality traits may be inherited more often than previously thought. For example, a couple may be mild, quiet people and have raised several children who are all like themselves except for one. The exception is a child who is loud, aggressive, and temperamental. Mom and Dad search their hearts wondering where they went wrong, never realizing those traits are embedded in the child's genes, and the characteristics inherited from a distant ancestor.

When a young fiancee says, "I don't like his family, but it doesn't matter, I'm not marrying them," it's time to worry. You do marry your spouse's family. The person you choose to spend your life with is a composite of his or her family's social experience and **genetic** (kinship) history. Your spouse may

1

not currently manifest undesirable traits, but with the wrong stimuli or pressures, could revert to inherited or learned ways of coping. By analyzing lovable characteristics along with any faults of the prospective in-laws, a couple can face potential problems and address questions about the future.

To isolate the individual from his kinship group and family in the name of love is to bury one's head in the sand. The apple doesn't fall far from the tree, they say, and the prickly pear tree produces only prickly pears.

How the family got started

By the act of being born we acquire a family, and the unifying ingredient of family life is kinship. Like most people, we probably don't think much about (or sometimes of) this group of Homo sapiens, or how they impact upon us. Oh, we may occasionally wonder how we got stuck with a particularly motley crew when John Doe down the street got all the winners, but that's about it.

Kinship ties probably began when our early ancestors entered the caves. **Paternal** (through the father) kinship was late in developing. A female had no way of knowing who fathered her child, and the male was unaware of his role in procreation, because sex was not understood as relevant to reproduction. With no estrous period (a specific time when an animal is in heat), the human female was available to the male at whim, and the long gestation removed the moment of conception a considerable distance from birth. Children were tremendously important to the small bands of struggling humanity, so birth was more significant than conception. Out of necessity, **matrilineal** (through the mother) kinship was the only form observed.

If an imaginary female named Ana had scratched her family tree on the cave wall, she would have provided an idea of how cognate (related on the mother's side) kinship was observed (figure 1).

As long as Ana's daughters produced females, Ana's line of descent remained recognizably intact. If the great-granddaughter produced only sons, the ability to trace Ana's line would cease. Remember the link between Ana and her offspring could only be traced through females descended from her.

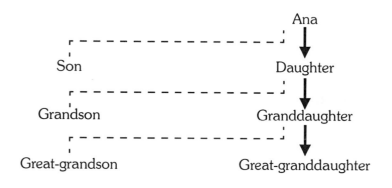

Figure 1 • Cognate kinship family tree

A new. theory concludes that every person living today is descended from one African female who walked the earth 140,000 to 280,000 years ago.

A peculiarity in cell structure permits only women to pass one class of genes, carried by mitochondrial DNA, to offspring. University of California professor Allan C. Wilson says, "Each of us, men and women, got our mitochondrial DNA only from our mother, and she from her mother, and her mother from her mother, all the way back."

Consider the implications. We may not be sisters and brothers, but we are at least fiftieth cousins to every other person on earth today.

Enter the patriarchy

Man, never long content on the sidelines, became aware of his role in reproduction sometime during the neolithic era. This realization may have been the catalyst which made him recognize he possessed some amazing attributes: a voice capable of communication, an ability by virtue of his strength to control the females and children, and most important, the capability to create his "own" offspring.

Equality of roles may have been the norm when the male role in fertilization was unknown, but if so, existing social structure changed, probably once man realized his contribution in begetting children. Picture early man whooping and hollering and carrying on, laughing and dancing and singing: "Me, me, I did it," he shouts to the moon. See the female sitting near the fire, mouth agape, wondering what all the commotion is about, never suspecting that her way of life has been totally altered.

The male pauses, looks about, considers the act which he has so freely shared with the other males, and suddenly realizes the need to restrict particular females to himself. How else to know if the child from a woman's womb was the seed of his loins? Patriarchy and the male ego were born.

Concurrently, the patiarchal "family" unit began to co-operate with other embryonic groups. Small bands joined with other "families" to form **clans**. Clans coalesced into **tribes**.

Phratries are large kinship alliances within a tribe of clans. A smaller, more cohesive kindred group within a phratry is called a **sib** (or **sept**), which consists of all persons descended from a real or supposed ancestor. The Old English word "sibb," meaning kinship or kinsman, is the root word of sib and also of **sibling** (brother or sister).

The important role of kinship continuously developed and enlarged. Kinship determined to which family, sib, sept, clan, phratry, and tribe one belonged, and with whom one could mate. Where **endogamy** (breeding within the social group) had been practical, **exogamy** (breeding outside the basic social group) became possible and preferable.

Perhaps the first sexual taboo was invented when tribal leaders needed ways to prevent excessive inbreeding in the interest of survival; therefore mating with certain relatives (incest) was forbidden. How better to control male and female sex drive than to channel it outward in the direction best suited for the union of diverse, yet similar, groups?

Nutrition improved when humans settled down to farm, and the world experienced a population explosion. Human development took a giant leap forward when **outbreeding** (bringing new blood into the kinship line) became possible on a grand scale. As the population increased, so did the possible number of mates from which to choose. It became absolutely necessary to have a way of ensuring the incest taboo was not broken. "Rememberers" were trained to commit family information to memory and, at the time of any sexual pairing, were called forth to recite the ancestral line of the couple. If all went well and no impediment was found, the couple was united by whatever rites of passage were prescribed.

Monogamy and the male line

How was man to insure the paternity of a particular child, especially a son, and know the identity of all progeny born into his family unless he carefully guarded the women with whom he mated? Like a small child just beginning to understand the idea of "mine," man's possessiveness now demanded **monogamy** (having only one mate) from the females associated with him. The patriarchal kinship system functioned well only if strict control was maintained over female sexual activity. So, man got busy and did just that. He veiled, girdled, spied upon, and cloistered the women in his family.

Where kinship had previously been traced by cognate descent (female lineage), **agnatic** descent (male lineage) became the accepted form. Man's feelings of superiority became entrenched in secular and religious laws, and marriage became the method by which man determined the offspring who would be designated his legal heirs.

2 • Marriage

Marriage

The first step to marriage begins when a man and a woman make a personal decision to blend their lives together for the purposes of emotional and financial support, and to raise their children within a legally recognized, nurturing network of family life.

By marriage, a couple creates a family (a legal continuation of their respective kinship lines) and enters regulated society. Marriage determines lawful unions, designates a father, and legitimizes the children. Any child born during the marriage is given legal recognition with all attendant rights, paternal ancestors, a family name, and a knowledge of his father's kinship connections.

Western law considers marriage a binding contract whereby one man and one woman with the legal capacity to enter such an agreement promise to live together for life, or until the marriage is legally terminated.

Once a couple makes the decision to marry, they are considered to be "promised" or "engaged." In the past, the engagement had greater legal ramifications than it does today. At one time, the person breaking the engagement could be sued for breach of promise. Most states have now abolished or limited such suits on the basis that marriage should never be entered into if either party has serious doubts.

Before they can be considered married, the couple must obtain a license from local authorities and go through a wedding ceremony. The following is a list of marital rites couples may choose, although some rites may not be legal in all states:

- The **ceremonial marriage** is a wedding performed in accordance with the law of the state in which it takes place.

- **Common-law marriage** is a private arrangement without a wedding ceremony or observance of legal requirements. If two persons who have the capacity to marry live together as husband and wife, assume marital duties and hold themselves out to others as married, they are usually considered married in the eyes of the law. Some states refuse to recognize this form of marriage.

- The **consensual marriage** requires spoken vows confirming the couple's intent. After the vows are spoken, the couple doesn't have to live together. The difference between common-law marriage and consensual marriage is that vows are not required in a common-law union. Again, some states do not recognize the consensual marriage.

- A **proxy marriage** requires special permission because it is allowed only when unusual circumstances keep the couple apart. Substitutes stand together and take the vows for the couple, who may be hundreds of miles away from each other. Most states discourage proxy marriages.

- Pssst—want to hear a secret? There's a marriage ceremony that most people aren't even aware of. It's called a **secret marriage**. A secret marriage is legal but quiet. It is a misdemeanor to publicize a secret marriage. You may ask who would want such a marriage? Well, persons in law enforcement often use this method to escape public attention that might lead a vindictive criminal to their doors. Couples who are not married but have allowed the public to think they are may wish to slip away and secretly formalize their union. The reasons for a secret ceremony are as varied as the couples who seek it. It's a binding and legal marriage, and can only be dissolved by the same legal process as is required by divorce. Sorry, there is no secret divorce. If you would like to consider a secret marriage, check with the proper authorities in your state. Sometimes the process is so hush-hush, it's difficult to find a magistrate who knows about it. If your reasons are compelling, keep trying.

Other cultures have their own forms of marriage. For example, in some parts of India and Sri Lanka, couples may contract a **benna marriage**, whereby the husband enters the wife's kinship group and has little authority in the household.

In ancient Rome, **coemptio marriages** symbolized the sale of a woman to a man and brought her under his power. Women frequently entered coemptio marriages to displace the jurisdiction of their legal guardians. Confarreation was another Roman rite that gave special sanctity to the marriage and conferred upon the husband absolute control over his wife, as if she were his daughter. A confarreation marriage could be dissolved only by a ceremony of **diffareation** (an ancient form of divorce).

Early Hebrews practiced a compulsory system known as the **levirate**, which required marriage of a widow to her late husband's brother or, in special circumstances, to her husband's heir. This arrangement attempted to ensure the continuation of the deceased man's bloodline.

When England's King Edward VIII decided to marry Wallis Warfield Simpson, a twice-divorced American, he proposed a **morganatic marriage**, whereby Mrs. Simpson would become his legal wife but would not hold the rank of queen. Any children they had would not succeed to Edward's titles, fiefs, or entailed property. The arrangement was rejected, and the King then abdicated his throne for, as he said, "the woman I love."

Who can marry?

There is a fundamental right to marry, which cannot be casually denied, and states must have valid reasons to prohibit the marriage of a particular couple. One of the most basic traditional requirements is that the couple consist of one man and one woman.

In 1989, Denmark became the first and, so far, the only country to allow "marriages" between homosexuals. The Danes Registered Partnership Law allows same-sex couples to be treated in the same manner as partners in traditional opposite-gender marriages. The homosexual partners may inherit from each other and are taxed the same as couples in traditional marriages. Basically, the only right denied the partners is the right to adopt children.

A few places in the United States (mostly towns near college campuses) have adopted domestic partnership policies that permit same-sex couples and unmarried heterosexuals to register their relationships in order to circumvent local ordinances that forbid unrelated persons to cohabit. So far, none of these alliances have been considered a real marriage as they are in Denmark, and they are under attack from conservative groups.

Hopefully, neither the prospective bride nor the prospective groom has a spouse hidden in the attic, or anywhere else for that matter. Marriage to a second person while still married to a first spouse is called **bigamy** and is considered a crime.

Polygamy (having more than one legal spouse at the same time) is forbidden in most of the Western world. At one time, the Church of Jesus Christ of Latter-day Saints (the Mormon Church) practiced polygyny (having more than one female spouse at the same time), but Mormon leaders bowed to legal and social pressure and banned the tradition about one hundred years ago. Some authorities claim the practice has simply gone underground and that polygynous marriages are now conducted in secret.

Islamic countries, which had permitted unlimited wives in the past, now generally permit men to have a maximum of four wives; on the other hand, the Nyimba tribe in Nepal allows **polyandry** (the marriage of one woman to several males). The Nyimba feel that men are more able to share a wife than women are to share a husband.

Age requirements

Forty-seven states and the District of Columbia allow any person 18 years old or over to marry without parental consent. In Mississippi and Puerto Rico both the man and woman must be 21.

Minors of a certain age may usually marry with parental permission, or if the bride is pregnant. In Georgia, parental consent isn't required at any age if the woman is pregnant or has a living child. In Kentucky and West Virginia, there is no minimum age for marriage if the parents consent.

Marriage to relatives

A Man may not marry his Mother.
Prayer Book 1662

Whether or not closely related couples may marry depends upon the degree of kinship and where they live. Every state forbids marriage to parents, siblings, uncles, aunts, nieces, nephews, and anyone in the grand generation (i.e., grandparent, grandaunt, granduncle), including illegitimate and half-blood relatives of the same degrees. Pennsylvania, which permits marriage to a great-grandparent, is the only state that allows marriage between an ancestor and a direct descendant.

Vermont recently dealt with a case in which an 86-year-old man wanted to marry his 65-year-old niece. After a doctor testified that the couple couldn't produce children, legislators passed an act which didn't set legal precedent, but did permit the elderly couple to marry.

In most states, first cousins (the respective children of siblings) can't marry, although first-cousin marriages are permitted in Wisconsin if the female is 55 years or older. Sometimes the marital ban is extended to first cousins once removed, certain in-laws and certain step-relatives. A new law in Massachusetts allows a woman to marry her father-in-law, but does not allow a man to marry his mother-in-law.

If a couple were too closely related to marry legally but married without knowing that fact, their marriage would be **voidable**. A voidable marriage is one that didn't initially meet the legal requirements of the state in which it was performed. Although marriage to someone in the forbidden degrees of kinship is considered a crime, the law isn't likely to prosecute unless someone complains.

There are several cases pending around the country where complainants have spoken—loud and clear. A father, separated from his infant daughter, later met and married her. Father and daughter claim they didn't know their familial status and have no plans to void the marriage. Shocked relatives say the couple certainly did know, and that even if they didn't then, they do now. And those relatives want them to stop living together— right now! Various kin have filed incest charges.

In 1986, Great Britain voided several of England's multitudinous civil incest prohibitions. Previously, certain affinial (in-law) relatives were forbidden to marry. Under the new provisions, a person may now marry a stepparent, a step-grandparent, a stepchild, or a stepgrandchild provided both parties are at least 21 years old at the time of the marriage— and provided the younger person wasn't treated as a "child of the family" prior to the age of 18. Marriage between a parent-in-law and a child-in-law is valid, provided both of the parties are over 21, and the child and the other parent of the child are both dead. For example: Mary and her father-in-law, John, wish to marry. Mary's husband (John's child) and Mary's mother-in-law (John's wife) must both have died before Mary and John can marry.

There is a question as to whether adopted siblings can marry. Two midwestern children adopted by the same family say civil incest laws shouldn't apply to them, because they are not blood kin. The court has ruled they are legally considered the same as biological brother and sister and therefore cannot marry. The couple hopes to have the adoption annulled; an annulment would clear the yellow-brick road to marriage.

In other parts of the world, close-kin nuptials are looked upon, in some cases, as an obligation. Muslim and Hindu societies have the highest incidences of intra-family marriages; first-cousin weddings are quite common. Orthodox Jews often marry first cousins.

People who wish to marry relatives should seek genetic counseling if there is a history of inherited diseases within the family. Scientists have identified certain ailments that tend to be associated with close-kin marriages, such as spina bifida, cleft palates, hip abnormalities, heart deformities, some blood diseases, and certain types of dwarfism.

Other premarital requirements

One of the first things a couple must do is apply for a marriage license from the appropriate governmental office. There may be a waiting period before the wedding can take place.

Before the license is granted, couples may be required to have premarital counseling and/or medical examinations, including blood tests to determine if they are free of venereal diseases. Idaho doesn't require a medical examination, but wants proof of rubella (German measles) immunity, presumably because rubella during pregnancy has been shown to damage the fetus.

Couples in Michigan are no longer required to have a blood test, but must present a certificate of Acquired Immune Deficiency Syndrome (AIDS) education. Couples in Louisiana and Illinois must be tested for AIDS. If evidence of a sexually transmitted disease is found, some states deny a license, while others require the infected person to disclose the results to the partner prior to the marriage.

Who performs the ceremony?

Only persons recognized by the state can perform valid marriage ceremonies. A list of approved government officials is available from local county courthouses. Wedding ceremonies may also be conducted by licensed and/or ordained ministers, priests, or rabbis.

Where?

There are no restrictions on where a couple may choose to tie the knot. Weddings have been conducted in airplanes (one couple exchanged vows during a free-falling sky dive), aboard ships, under water, in fast-food restaurants, in hot-air balloons, and on rapid transit systems. The most frequently encountered impediment to having the ceremony in an unusual or dangerous place is the difficulty of convincing a duly approved person to perform the ceremony there.

Premarital agreements

Eight states have community property laws giving spouses equal ownership of all possessions brought to or acquired by either party during the marriage—which brings up the subject of premarital (also called "prenuptial" or "antenuptial") agreements. A premarital agreement is a contract signed prior to the marriage detailing issues such as support, distribution of wealth, and division of property in the event of divorce or the death of one of the parties.

Alabama, California, Colorado, Florida, Illinois, Indiana, Louisiana, and Virginia recognize premarital agreements, although their courts scrutinize such agreements to make sure they are just and reasonable. Kansas, Michigan, and Minnesota refuse to honor premarital agreements, although Michigan is in the process of reevaluating its stance. Many of the courts that won't enforce premarital agreements will sometimes consider such documents as guides when making their decisions.

Valid premarital contracts must be voluntary and must be entered only after a full and fair financial disclosure by both parties. If important information is withheld, such as the value of one's estate, the agreement can be set aside. And "voluntary" doesn't mean the bride or groom is met at the chapel door by an attorney and either signs the agreement or cancels the wedding. Voluntary means that both parties have had time to study the document and to consult with their personal attorneys. Anyone considering the use of a premarital agreement certainly should seek legal counsel.

Basic marital rights

Over the years, states have modified their laws to reflect the changing nature of marriage. At one time the law assumed that the husband provided financial support and that the wife maintained the home. Today, such gender-specific requirements or assumptions have given way to the designation of a "dependent spouse," who may be either male or female.

A spouse has a legal right to sexual intimacy with a mate. Although that right can't be forced upon the reluctant spouse (marital rape has become a big issue), after considering age and health, the courts do uphold reasonable demands while recognizing that a marriage at that stage is probably doomed anyway.

A married man is considered by law to be the father of any children born to his wife during the duration of their marriage. By marrying, he in effect declares that he will accept, as his own, any children born to his wife during the marriage.

Historically, the husband has had the right to choose the family residence. At one time, the wife might have been charged with desertion if she refused to accompany her husband when he changed residences. Now, courts are increasingly acknowledging that a married woman may live anywhere she wants to; however, in Michigan, an old law allows the prosecution of married couples for not living together.

If one spouse gives the other expensive gifts and then wants them back, the recipient doesn't have to return them. And neither spouse may invite live-in guests (including parents) without the other's express permission. Short-term visitors need not meet with a spouse's approval.

And no fair hitting. Spouses aren't allowed to physically abuse each other. That hasn't always been true. At one time the "rule of thumb" prevailed: A man could legally beat his wife if the weapon he used had a circumference no greater than that of his thumb.

In 1978-79, more than half the states adopted, revised, or had pending legislation dealing with domestic violence and protection of battered spouses. The law also frowns on mental cruelty, which is harder to prove, since the bruises don't show.

Infidelity is grounds for divorce in most states; however, if the spouse discovers and forgives the adultery, and welcomes the offender back into the marital bed, the aggrieved person can't later sue over the original act. In that case, the mate is said to have "condoned," or legally accepted, the spouse's action.

Divorce

Tammy Wynette became rich and famous singing a song called *Stand by Your Man*. But one day, Tammy got D-I-V-O-R-C-E-D (another country/western offering). In some countries, divorce is out of the question. Ireland, the Philippines, and Malta are among the few countries that allow annulment (dissolution of a marriage that wasn't valid in the first place) but not divorce.

When a divorce is granted, there is a marked effort to have an equitable division of property. Lately, the trend is to consider all assets, not just real estate and money. If one spouse has devoted time and energy in helping the other obtain an advanced college degree, judges often put a dollar value on the potential earnings and order a portion of those earnings paid to the helpful spouse.

In Merrie Olde England, divorce was a simpler matter. A man could legally sell his wife. He simply tied a halter around her neck, marched her off to the local market, and offered her to the highest bidder. In the last recorded case, back in 1832, a Carlisle farmer accepted 20 shillings and a Newfoundland pup in exchange for his wife.

Wives were not allowed to sell their husbands. But an old law in Wales permitted a wife to divorce her husband if he had bad breath.

Live-ins

> *I never will marry. Ill be no man's wife. I will remain single for the rest of my life.*
>
> Popular folk song

In our country today, 2 million couples live together without marriage. Their obligations to each other fall into a legal no-man's land.

At one time, most states followed the English practice of recognizing common-law marriages. If a couple lived as husband and wife and held themselves out to society as husband and wife, the state accepted them as a married couple. Many states have outlawed common-law marriages. However, if a couple meets the requirements of a common-law marriage in a state that permits such marriages, the marriage is recognized as valid anywhere the couple may go. Such marriages must be dissolved by a legal divorce.

Alabama, Colorado, the District of Columbia, Georgia, Idaho, Iowa, Kansas, Montana, Ohio, Oklahoma, Pennsylvania, Rhode Island, South Carolina, and Texas recognize common-law marriages. Several states accept common-law marriages that were entered into prior to specific dates.

In Michigan, as in 11 other states, cohabitation between unmarried couples is illegal. In Alabama and South Carolina, an individual can't live with a person who is married to someone else.

From the number of "palimony" suits lately, one might assume that living-together couples aren't immune from the same difficulties as married people. Financial experts advise unmarried couples to plan ahead for the day when the arrangement sours. They say couples need a written agreement specifying the assets each party brought to the liaison and what happens to property acquired together, as well as an agreement to put both names on any leases unless cohabitation is illegal in their particular state.

In reality, there are considerable liabilities to living together. Live-ins can't file joint tax returns, can't automatically inherit from each other, and do not qualify for employer-sponsored medical insurance for spouses. (Some large corporations are privately recognizing long-term, live-in arrangements if the two parties—and in some cases homosexuals qualify—can prove their commitment to each other.)

Courts occasionally apply the same principles to cohabiting couples as they do to married people, but only on a case-by-case basis. Perhaps the best place for living together is Oregon, where live-ins have an equal interest in property.

However, be forewarned. While some states condone living-together arrangements, the Social Security Administration refuses to pay spousal benefits to unmarried couples.

Obviously, couples should familiarize themselves with the laws and social acceptance of their communities before making the decision to live together.

* * *

By complying with the laws of society, observing the customs of your faith (considered optional by those who do not value the role of religion), and confronting myriad responsibilities, you are ready to begin your own family and to legally continue your kinship line. You and your spouse will leave your **family of orientation** (the family of your parents and relatives), and become a **family of procreation** (the family created by marriage). By marriage, you acquire a new set of relatives, who will be your **family of affinity**—the birth group of your spouse.

LEGAL MARRIAGE AGE[1]					RELATIVES YOU CAN'T MARRY[2]
STATE	Without Parental Consent		With Parental Consent		
	Male	Female	Male	Female	
Alabama	18	18	14	14	Stepparent, stepchild, son-in-law, daughter-in-law
Alaska	18	18	16, 14[3]	16, 14[3]	
Arizona	18	18	16	16	First cousin
Arkansas	18	18	17	16	First cousin
California	18	18	___[4]	___[4]	
Colorado	18	18	16	16	
Connecticut	18	18	16	16	Stepparent, stepchild
Delaware	18	18	18	16	First cousin
District of Columbia	18	18	16	16	Stepparent, stepchild, stepgrandparent, father-in-law, mother-in-law, daughter-in-law, son in law, grandchild's spouse, spouse's grandparent or grandchild
Florida	18	18	16	16	
Georgia	18	18	16	16	Stepparent, stepchild, father-in-law, mother-in-law, son-in-law, daughter-in-law, stepgrandparent, stepgrandchild
Hawaii	18	18	16	16	
Idaho	18	18	16	16	First Cousin
Illinois	18	18	16	16	First Cousin
Indiana	18	18	17	17	First Cousin
Iowa	18	18	16	16	First Cousin, stepparent, stepchild, grandchild's spouse, father in law, mother-in-law, son-in-law, daughter-in-law

LEGAL MARRIAGE AGE[1]				RELATIVES YOU CAN'T MARRY[2]
STATE	Without Parental Consent		With Parental Consent	
	Male	Female	Male	Female	

STATE	Male	Female	Male	Female	RELATIVES YOU CAN'T MARRY[2]
Kansas	18	18	___[4]	___[5]	First cousin
Kentucky	18	18	___[4]	___[5]	First cousin, first cousin once removed
Louisiana	18	18	18	16	First cousin
Maine	18	18	16	16	Stepparent, stepchild, spouse of a grandparent or grandchild, father-in-law, mother-in-law, son-in-law, daughter-in-law, spouse's grandparent or grandchild
Maryland	18	18	16	16	Spouse's parent, grandparent, child or grandchild; spouse of parent, grandparent, child or grandchild
Massachusetts	18	18	___[4]	___[4]	Stepparent, stepchild, stepgrandparent, father-in-law, mother-in-law, son-in-law, daughter-in-law
Michigan	18	18	18	16	First cousin
Minnesota	18	18	16	18	First cousin
Mississippi	___[6]	___[6]	___[6]	___[6]	Stepparent, stepchild, first cousin, father-in-law, mother-in-law, son-in-law, daughter-in-law
Missouri	18	18	15	15	First cousin
Montana	18	18	16	16	First cousin
Nebraska	19	18	17	17	First cousin
Nevada	18	18	16	16	First cousin

LEGAL MARRIAGE AGE[1]				RELATIVES YOU CAN'T MARRY[2]
STATE	Without Parental Consent		With Parental Consent	
	Male	Female	Male	Female	

STATE	Male	Female	Male	Female	RELATIVES YOU CAN'T MARRY[2]
New Hampshire	18	18	14	13	Spouse of parent or child, first cousin
New Jersey	18	18	16	16	
New Mexico	18	18	16	16	
New York	18	18	16	14[3]	
North Carolina	18	18	16	16	Double first cousin
North Dakota	18	18	16	16	First cousin
Ohio	18	18	18	16	First cousin
Oklahoma	18	18	16	16	First cousin
Oregon	18	18	17	17	First cousin
Pennsylvania	18	18	16	16	Stepparent, stepchild, first cousin, son-in-law, daughter-in-law[7]
Rhode Island	18	18	18	16	Spouse's parent, grandparent or grandchild (except as permitted by religious law)
South Carolina	18	18	16	14	Spouse's parent, grandparent, child, or grandchild; spouse of parent, grandparent, child or grandchild
South Dakota	18	18	16	16	First cousin, stepparent, stepchild
Tennessee	18	18	16	16	Stepparent, stepchild, stepgrandchild, grandnephew, grandniece
Texas	18	18	14	14	
Utah	18	18	14	14	First cousin

LEGAL MARRIAGE AGE[1]					RELATIVES YOU CAN'T MARRY[2]
STATE	Without Parental Consent		With Parental Consent		
	Male	Female	Male	Female	
Vermont	18	18	16, 14[3]	16, 14[3]	
Virginia	18	18	16	16	
Washington	18	18	17	17	First cousin
West Virginia	18	18	18	16	First cousin, double first cousin
Wisconsin	18	18	16	16	First cousin unless female 55 years or older
Wyoming	19	19	16	16	First cousin

[1]Almost all states have established 18 as the minimum age at which a person may obtain a marriage license. Persons below that age must generally have the consent of their parents under oath. Court approval may also be required to waive the minimum age at which a couple may marry, regardless of parental consent, if the female is pregnant or if birth out of wedlock has already occurred.

[2]In every state it is illegal for a man to marry his sister, half sister, mother, daughter, granddaughter, grandmother, great-grandmother (see exception in Pennsylvania), aunt or niece. It is also illegal for a woman to marry her brother, half-brother, stepson, great-grandfather (see exception in Pennsylvania), niece or nephew.

[3]With court permission.

[4]No statutory minimum age: both court permission and parental consent are required.

[5]Commissioner of human services has authority to waive this requirement.

[6]No statutory minimum age. Males and females require a court order. Other conditions may apply. Check with proper authority.

[7]In Pennsylvania, there is no provision against marrying your great-grandparent (see footnote 2)

COMMON-LAW MARRIAGE

State	Are Common-Law Marriages Allowed?*	State	Are Common-Law Marriages Allowed?*
Alabama	Yes	Iowa	Yes
Alaska	No	Kansas	Yes
Arizona	No	Kentucky	No
Arkansas	No	Louisiana	No
California	No	Maine	No
Colorado	No	Maryland	No
Connecticut	No	Massachusetts	No
Delaware	No	Michigan	No, unless entered before Jan. 1, 1957
District of Columbia	Yes	Minnesota	No, unless entered before April 26, 1941
Florida	No, unless entered before Jan. 1, 1968	Mississippi	No, unless entered before April 5, 1956
Georgia	Yes	Missouri	No, unless entered before March 31, 1921
Hawaii	No	Montana	Yes
Idaho	Yes	Nebraska	No, unless entered before 1923
Illinois	No, unless entered before June 30, 1905	Nevada	No, unless entered before March 29, 1943
Indiana	No, unless entered before 1958	New Hamphsire	No

COMMON-LAW MARRIAGE

State	Are Common-Law Marriages Allowed?*	State	Are Common-Law Marriages Allowed?*
New Jersey	No, unless entered before Dec. 1, 1939	South Dakota	No, unless entered before July 1, 1959
New Mexico	No	Tennessee	No
New York	No, unless entered before April 29, 1933	Texas	Yes
North Carolina	No	Utah	No
North Dakota	No, since 1890	Vermont	No
Ohio	Yes	Virginia	No
Oklahoma	Yes	Washington	No
Oregon	No	West Virginia	No
Pennsylvania	Yes	Wisconsin	No, unless entered before 1917
Rhode Island	Yes	Wyoming	No
South Carolina	Yes		

* All states must recognize a common-law marriage that has been entered into in another state and is considered valid in that state.

3 • Kinship Groups

Oh, Lord: help me. If you don't, I'll ask my uncle in New York.

Jewish folk saying

Belonging to a family

Families are based on kinship; members belong by blood (birth), by affinity (marriage), or through the courts (adoption). In adoption, the adoptee becomes a legally accepted member of the biological family with the same rights of inheritance as a person born to the family. One exception may be the inheritance of an ancestral estate which, by prior will or entail, must descend to a "blood" relative.

Some families extend a special affection to special friends under the umbrella of **fictive kinship**. These people are treated with deference and respect even to the point of using familial terms when addressing them.

Sometimes a person lives with a family but isn't a member by blood, marriage, or adoption. In this situation, the designation is **foster-child** or **foster-parent**. (Technically, the term parent is reserved for one's mother and father, but general usage has enlarged the meaning to include grandmother and grandfather, and others acting in the parental stead.)

Some primitive societies, in their innate wisdom, made use of foster relationships by traditionally sending children to live with maternal or paternal uncles and aunts. The idea seemed to be that by removing the emotional anxiety felt by the natural parents, the child more easily matured.

Types of family

In the United States, family life is defined by the **nuclear family**. Married couples with their children establish separate homes from and are financially independent of the couple's parents. However, kin ties are still extremely important.

If married children and their offspring live with the parents, the family is called an **extended family**. An extended family also includes aunts, uncles, and cousins along with grandparents, grandchildren, and others even if they live in separate homes. Many cultures assiduously maintain extended family ties.

Many countries, including Scotland and Ireland, recognize a large kinship group known as a **clan**. They maintain a strong interest in preserving clan history and traditions.

Tribal societies such as those of the Middle, Near, and Far East, plus some Latin countries, place greater emphasis on the extended family than do societies consisting mainly of nuclear families. It's usual in tribal societies to receive widows, divorced people, or never-married women into the bosom of the family, and to provide homes for elderly relatives.

When parents equally share the responsibility of a family, the unit is called an **equalitarian** or **egalitarian family**. Depending on which marital partner you speak to, such a family may or may not exist.

If a male heads the family, it's a **patriarchal family**. A **matriarchal family** is led by a female. A dictatorship is a family ruled by a two-year-old child. Just ask any couple that has one!

The **stepfamily** comes into existence when a divorced or widowed parent remarries. The new spouse becomes a stepparent to the children of the former marriage. Folklore has traditionally maligned the stepmother; consider the reputations of the stepmothers of Cinderella and Snow White. Conversely, stepchildren usually are portrayed as beautiful, lovable, and perfect. According to the stories, Cinderella and Snow White never left their clothes lying around the castle, refused to eat their dinner, or wrecked the family coach, or we might better understand the actions of the substitute parent.

Offspring from the couple's prior marriages become stepbrothers and stepsisters. Children who share a single biological parent are **half-brothers** and **half-sisters**.

Ascents and descents

Kinship is figured **bilaterally** in the United States, which means an individual is affiliated with and descent traced through relatives on both the maternal and the paternal sides. Normally, the kinship circle is confined to a small group of kin consisting of grandparents, aunts, uncles, and cousins. The members of this group are considered one's kindred.

Kinship boundaries expand and contract depending on what some people call the "rich relative syndrome (RRS)." Under RRS, expansion in the kindred network allows inclusion of a shirt-tail third cousin once removed who is rich or famous, and contraction occurs when infamy rears its ugly head in the form of a first cousin.

In some societies, a descent group is traced **unilineally** through either the mother or the father. Rights and responsibilities are more clearly delineated than in Western societies using bilateral descent.

Obviously, the study of kinship pays particular attention to **ascents** and **descents**, from which we derive **ancestors** and descendants. Ascents (up from the self or ego) and descents (down from an ancestor) are of two types: **lineal** and **collateral**.

Lineal

Lineal descent is a direct or straight line from parent or grandparent to child or grandchild. **Lineal ascent** is from the self or ego in a straight line to parent or grandparent (figure 2).

Lineal descents/ascents are **immediate** and **mediate**. An immediate lineal descent is from parent to child, and mediate lineal descent is from grandparent to grandchild. A descent is immediate only when there is no intervening link between ancestor and descendant.

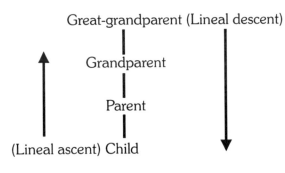

Figure 2 • Lineal descent and ascent

Collateral

In addition to grandparents, parents bequeath to their children another group of relatives known as collaterals; the kinship line is oblique rather than straight.

Collateral blood relatives are neither descendants nor ancestors in the strictest sense of the word. The term collateral kindred is used to designate brothers, sisters, uncles, aunts, nieces, nephews, and cousins. Collaterals descend from a common antecedent but can neither ascend to nor descend from other collateral relatives.

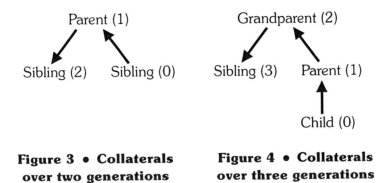

Figure 3 • Collaterals over two generations

Figure 4 • Collaterals over three generations

Figure 3 shows the connection between collaterals. Starting with one sibling (0), the line ascends to the common ancestor and descends to the other sibling (2).

In figure 4 the line ascends from child (0), to parent (1), to grandparent (2), and down to parent's sibling (3). The numbers in parentheses represent the **degree of relationship**, which is explained more fully in the next chapter.

Three families at once

Kinship in the first instance is that which belongs to one by birth, and refers to origin or descent, birthright, or inheritance. Kinship is based on the biological blood we share with others. When someone says, "Blood is thicker than water!" they proclaim their first loyalties lie with family members.

Our place in the family structure is determined by the degree (amount) of blood we share with others. But we can simultaneously belong to three different kinship groups. Life begins in a **family of orientation** (parents, their offspring, and other parental relatives). When we marry, we establish a **family of procreation** (for the purpose of having children), and through our spouse we gain a **family of affinity** (the kinship group to which our spouse belongs). These three families deserve a new chapter.

4 • Our Three families

(Aunt Alexandra) never let a chance escape her to point out the shortcomings of other tribal groups to the greater glory of our own, a habit that amused Jem rather than annoyed him: "Aunty better watch how she talks—scratch most folks in Maycomb and they're kin to us."
Harper Lee, *To Kill a Mockingbird*

Family of orientation

By birth, we belong to a family of orientation; the family of our parents and their relatives. We are who we are because they are who they are. From them we inherit our physical and emotional characteristics such as disposition, eye color, body structure, and facial features. Blame those protruding teeth or that big nose on some long-forgotten ancestor if it makes you feel any better, but don't forget to thank them for a beautiful smile, flirtatious dimple, or gorgeous red hair.

The family of orientation is the only family that can't be chosen. We carry the inherited genes around like so much baggage, and wouldn't mind a bit if parts of it were lost en route. Even when we believe we have successfully performed self-surgery on certain characteristics, the child or grandchild arrives as a reminder that the tendencies are waiting in the wings.

Siblings-german (children born of the same parents–the word "german" means full or whole, and is becoming obsolete) are the closest blood relatives, with the possible exception of **identical twins** (children conceived simultaneously as a

31

division of the ovum.) **Fraternal twins** (children conceived from separate ova) are no closer genetically than children individually born. See figure 5.

Father + Mother

Son ◄—— Siblings ——► Daughter   (Full brother/sister)

Figure 5 • Full siblings or siblings-german

Within the family of orientation we first look to our parents, and to their parents. From self or ego, the direct line ascends to parents (the **parental** generation), grandparents (the **grand** generation), great-grandparents (the **great-grand** generation), adding a **great** for each preceding generation.

Patrilineal ascendancy is through the father, and matrilineal through the mother. Your father's relatives are paternal kin, your mother's relatives are maternal kin. You are a descendant of these relatives, and conversely they are your ancestors (figure 6).

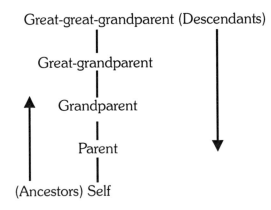

Great-great-grandparent (Descendants)

Great-grandparent

Grandparent

Parent

(Ancestors) Self

Figure 6 • Direct line of ascent/descent

Degrees of relationship

The chart of consanguinity (figure 7) shows the **degrees of relationship** between Self (0) and other relatives. Attorneys use charts similar to this one to determine next of kin and degree of relationship for purposes of distribution of property in intestate cases (where someone has died without leaving a will). They also use these charts to determine the degrees within which marriage is prohibited (incest), and as a basis for allowing certain relatives to testify against each other.

Notice that some relatives have the same degree of relationship to Self. For example: grandnephews/nieces (4), first cousins (4), granduncles/aunts (4) and great-great-grandparents (4). All of these relatives are in the fourth **degree of kinship** (or **consanguinity**) to Self.

The arrows linking Self to descendants and ancestors indicates lineal relatives. All others are collaterals.

Confused? Don't worry! In the rest of this section we'll work gradually through what all the relationships are called and what the names mean.

Aunts and uncles

The brother or sister of your parents is respectively your uncle (male) or your aunt (female). In some societies, paternal uncles and aunts have more status than maternal uncles and aunts.

At one time an unrelated woman addressed as aunt would have been insulted. The term implied that she was an old crone or a prostitute. Evolution has worked its magic and the term is now perfectly respectable.

On the other hand, an uncle was a man whose wisdom and help were sought. A children's game sometimes ended with the vanquished forced to cry "Uncle!" This in effect acknowledged the winner as wiser and definitely stronger than the loser. Crying uncle was the only way to get a bully off one's chest. Do children of today still do that?

"Uncle" was also a slang term for pawnbrokers. That makes sense if a person had no real uncle to turn to in time of trouble.

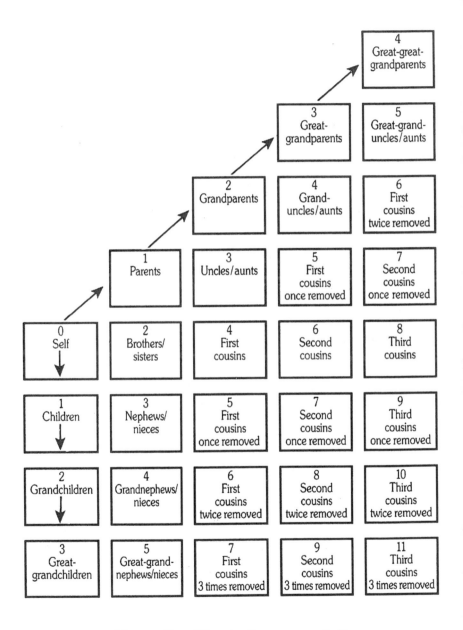

Figure 7 • Chart of consanguinity

Then, of course, there is Uncle Sam, the cartoon symbol of the United States. He's a skinny, goateed fellow dressed in the national colors who tells the populace exactly what the government expects of them. To "speak like a Dutch uncle" has come to mean giving someone a disciplinary talking-to. The same message from an aunt is known as nagging.

Nieces and nephews

You will be recognized by your uncle and aunt as either **niece** (female) or **nephew** (male).

"Nephew" is an interesting word which archaically meant grandson or any male descendant. The word is taken from French nepote and Latin *nepos*. Similarly, *"niece"* came via French from Latin *neptis*, meaning granddaughter. *Nepote* and *nepos* also contributed the word "nepotism." Nepotism means favoritism shown to nephews and other relatives by reason of consanguinity rather than merit. Nepotism is practiced more often in the private sector than in the public sector. However, we usually see more merit in our relatives than do outsiders. There are some people whose good qualities can only be recognized by relatives, particularly when there is pressure from Aunt Nellie to give Nephew Ned Nerd a job. After all, if you won't favor your relatives, who will? And look at it this way, if God hadn't wanted us to prefer our relatives, he wouldn't have given us any.

Incidentally, in some African tribal societies there is no word for aunt, uncle, or cousin. The children of your siblings are considered to be your children as though you had conceived them. You're expected to accept responsibility whenever there's a need. The children of siblings describe each other as brother and sister instead of "cousin." The children address as mother and father not only their biological parents, but the parental siblings.

Generations

Parents and their siblings belong to one generation and their respective offspring to another. In kinship, **one generation is**

a single step in the line of descent from an ancestor. A mother can give birth to two children twenty years apart, but the siblings will always be in the same kinship generation. This is unlike social generations, which are made up of persons of similar ages.

The example of siblings whose births are separated by many years demonstrates how a person belongs to several different generations simultaneously. By birth, children are bound together in their kinship generation, but each will grow up in vastly different social and work generations.

Regardless of the time span between siblings, neither the family titles nor the kinship generations change. A woman who finds herself giving birth about the same time as does her daughter or daughter-in-law bears a child who enters the world as an aunt or uncle to her new grandchild.

Greats and grands

The siblings of your grandparents will be your **grandaunts** and **granduncles**. It's a mistake to lump them in with the "greats." What does the term "great aunt" mean? Does it mean a sister of a grandparent or a sister of a great-grandparent? Mixing the generations causes confusion. Some reference books designate a grandaunt as a great aunt, which compounds the problem since we expect more accuracy from the experts.

With the grands and the greats, this is the sequence: **grand**parent, **great-grand**parent, **great-great-grand**parent. Continue adding a great for every preceding generation. The same follows for grandaunt and granduncle, and grandniece and grandnephew. After the grands come the great-grands.

- *Great-grand*uncles/aunts are siblings of *great-grand-parents*
- *Grand*uncles/aunts are siblings of *grand*parents
- Uncles/aunts are siblings of parents
- *Self*

Each line above represents one generation.

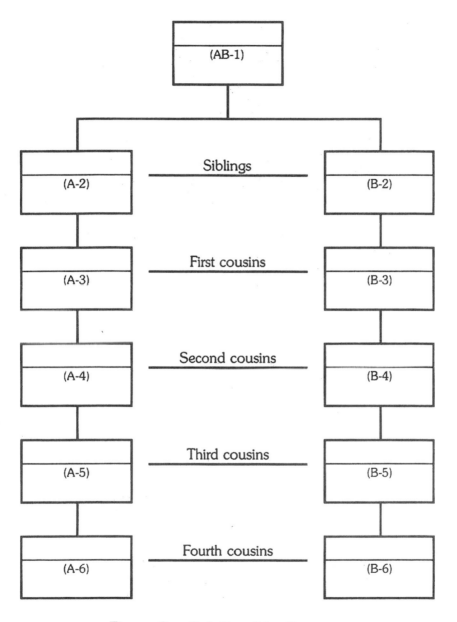

Figure 8 • Relationship diagram

Cousins

Cousins share a common grandparent, with the degree of cousin-ship dependent on how the grandparent is shared (figure 8).

- Siblings *share* a parent.
- First cousins *share* a grandparent.
- Second cousins *share* a great-grandparent.
- Third cousins *share* a great-great-grandparent.
- Fourth cousins *share* a great-great-great-grandparent.
- Fifth cousins *share* a great-great-great-great-grandparent (and so on).

Another way to determine cousins is to look at aunts and uncles. The children of your aunts and uncles are your **cousins-german** or **first cousins**. In figure 9, grandparent (2) is a common ancestor of the self, parent, aunt/uncle, and child.

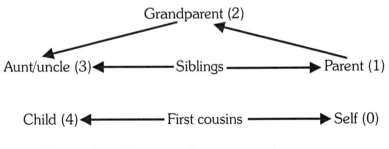

Figure 9 • First cousins, or cousins-german

Quarter cousins are properly in the **fourth degree** of consanguinity (that is, first cousins), but the term has come to express any remote degree of relationship, and even to bear an ironical significance in which it denotes a very trifling degree of kinship. Quarter is a term often corrupted to **cater**, which refers to the four spots on dice or cards.

The removes

If your first cousin has a child, the child becomes your **first cousin once removed**. The **removes** seem to create considerable difficulty. A question frequently asked is, "Removed from whom and to where?" No, it doesn't refer to the situation where someone demands, "Remove that child at once."

Simply put, removed means that a person belongs to a different kinship generation. A first cousin once removed is one generation removed from the source—a first cousin. Think of it as linguistic shorthand: "My first cousin once removed," instead of "My first cousin's child is one kinship generation removed from our original first cousin relationship."

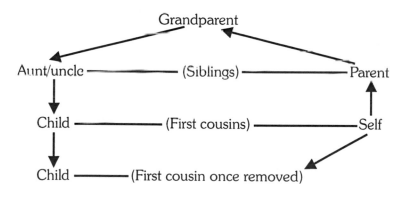

Figure 10 • First cousins once removed

For example, in figure 10 the sibling of Self's parent is Self's aunt or uncle. The child of the aunt or uncle is Self's first cousin. The child of Self's first cousin is a first cousin once removed to Self. Self's grandparent is the great-grandparent of Self's first cousin once removed. They are cousins by virtue of a shared grandparent by different degrees.

The child of Self's first cousin once removed is a first cousin twice removed (see figure 11). Each new generation will continue to be another step removed from the original first cousin relationship.

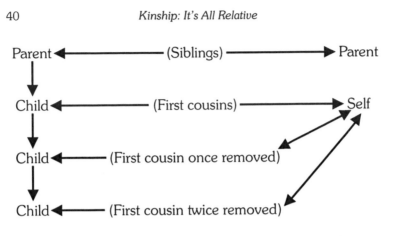

Figure 11 • First cousins twice removed

Ask yourself, "Who is John to me?" If you know that John's mother is your third cousin, then John is your third cousin once removed. If John is your third cousin once removed, one of your great-great-grandparents will be John's great-great-great-grandparent.

Calculating cousinhood

How does one acquire second cousins? By being the respective children of first cousins. In figure 11, Self had no children. Let's see what will happen if Self has a child (figure 12).

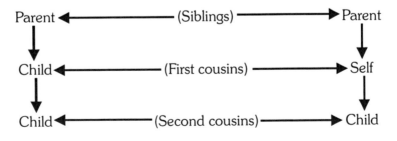

Figure 12 • Second cousins

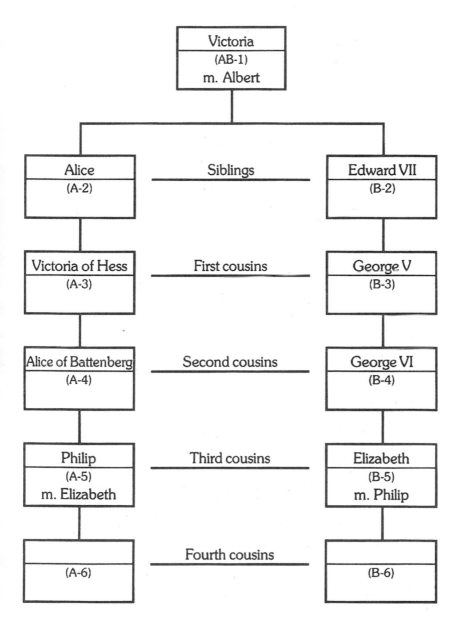

**Figure 13 • Relationship diagram for
Queen Elizabeth II and Prince Philip**

Relationship Table A

Relation-ship of A	AB-1	B-2	B-3	B-4	B-5	B-6
AB-1		Parents	Grandparent	Great-grandparent	Great-great-grandparent	Great-great-great-grandparent
A-2	Child	Brother/sister	Aunt/uncle	Grand-aunt/uncle	Great-grand-aunt/uncle	Great-great-grand-aunt/uncle
A-3	Grandchild	Niece/nephew	First cousin	First cousin once removed	First cousin twice removed	First cousin three times removed
A-4	Great-grandchild	Grand-niece/nephew	First cousin once removed	Second cousin	Second cousin once removed	Second cousin twice removed
A-5	Great-great-grandchild	Great-grand-niece/nephew	First cousin twice removed	Second cousin once removed	Third cousin	Third cousin once removed
A-6	Great-great-great-grandchild	Great-great-grandniece/nephew	First cousin three times removed	Second cousin twice removed	Third cousin once removed	Fourth cousin

1. To find the relationship of A to B, find the "A" code (e.g. A-4) of the individual, from the relationship diagram (figure 8).
2. Select the code in the left-hand column of the table above.
3. Read across the row to the desired column (e.g. B-5) to find the relationship.

Relationship Table B

Relation-ship of B	AB-1	A-2	A-3	A-4	A-5	A-6
B-1		Parents	Grandparent	Great-grandparent	Great-great-grandparent	Great-great-great-grandparent
B-2	Child	Brother/sister	Aunt/uncle	Grand-aunt/uncle	Great-grand-aunt/uncle	Great-great-grand-aunt/uncle
B-3	Grandchild	Niece/nephew	First cousin	First cousin once removed	First cousin twice removed	First cousin three times removed
B-4	Great-grandchild	Grand-niece/nephew	First cousin once removed	Second cousin	Second cousin once removed	Second cousin twice removed
B-5	Great-great-grandchild	Great-grand-niece/nephew	First cousin twice removed	Second cousin once removed	Third cousin	Third cousin once removed
B-6	Great-great-great-grandchild	Great-great-grandniece/nephew	First cousin three times removed	Second cousin twice removed	Third cousin once removed	Fourth cousin

4. To find the relationship of B to A, find the "B" code (e.g. B-4) of the individual, from the relationship diagram (figure 8).
5. Select the code in the left-hand column of the table above.
6. Read across the column to the desired row (e.g. A-5) to find the relationship.

Figure 14 • Relationship tables

Earlier we looked at another way to determine degrees of cousinhood through the grandparents. Let's review. Remember, **cousins are relatives who share a common grandparent.**

Children of first cousins are second cousins, and offspring of second cousins are third cousins. To take an example (figure 13), Queen Elizabeth II of England married her third cousin, Philip Mountbatten (Bartenberg). Elizabeth and Philip are related through the lineage of Queen Victoria, their common great-great-grandmother. This relationship places them in the eighth degree of consanguinity. The degree is calculated by starting with Elizabeth (0) and proceeding through the line of ascent to the nearest common progenitor, Victoria (4), and then down to the relative in question, Philip (8).

At various times in the past, this relationship might have been within the forbidden (incest) degrees for marriage purposes. It also means that Philip and Elizabeth are **third cousins once removed** to their own children.

Queen Victoria had nine children, and she judiciously arranged marriages for them with most of the royal families of Europe, so that an in-depth examination of her descendants reveals a jumble of kinship lines. You can use figure 14 to help you work out your own kinship lines.

Doubles, parallels and crosses

A unique relationship comes into existence when siblings of one family marry siblings of another family. For example, if the brothers Smith marry the sisters Jones, their offspring will be **double first cousins**. Genetically, their children will inherit from the same gene pool as if they were siblings. While regular first cousins share only one set of common ancestors, double first cousins share all lineal and collateral relatives. In addition to being double first cousins, the Smith/Jones children are also **parallel** (or **ortho**) **first cousins**.

Parallel cousins are the children of two brothers or two sisters. **Cross cousins** are the children of a brother and a sister. For example, my sister and I have children, therefore our children are cognate parallel cousins. My brother and I have children and our respective children are cross cousins (figure 15).

Arab Bedouin societies frequently place great importance upon the first male child of one brother having marital rights to female offspring of another brother. Cross cousin marriages do occur in Arabic societies but without the familial significance of agnatic parallel cousin marriages.

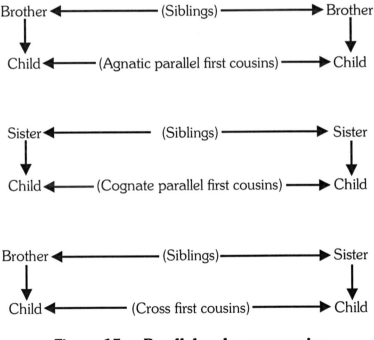

Figure 15 • Parallel and cross cousins

Cousins who aren't cousins

"Cousin" seems to be used when it's a bother to delve into more complicated family relationships. When the English Crown issues writs or other formal instruments, the word "cousin" signifies any peer of the degree of earl.

The practice of addressing an earl as "cousin" began when Henry IV, related to or allied with every earl then in the kingdom, wearied of trying to keep each earl in the proper degree of kinship. Henry was concerned about hurt feelings and their possible consequences if he miscalculated a single degree, whole or removed, so he solved the problem by addressing all of them as "Dear cousin." The tradition holds while the reason has become lost in antiquity.

Maybe some African families have the right idea. Be done with the whole jumble of aunts and uncles and cousins by degree. Just call some people mom and dad, and all the others brother and sister.

In conclusion

Grandparents and the greats, father, mother, aunts, uncles, and cousins by degree—these are the members of our family of orientation. There is no choice involved. We can't divorce them, although we can disinherit them. We can love them, leave them, hate them, need them, avoid them, ignore them, and pretend they don't exist . . . and nothing changes; blood remains the same.

We must take them as we get them, and they often hang about our necks like albatrosses, getting in our way and embarrassing us at every opportunity. But what would we do without them? We look in their faces and see ourselves and our children. They share our rites of passage: weddings, births, deaths, happy times, sad times, laughter, and tears. They sing our lullabies and recite our goodnight prayers. They are there for us, and we for them. To paraphrase Pogo from his home in the swamp, "We have met our kindred and they are us."

Family of procreation

When we marry, we enter a family of procreation. This family is created by choice. Many people have lived to regret in leisure a spouse chosen in haste. Whether or not a couple actually produce offspring doesn't alter the terminology of the kinship purpose. It's within this family, if all goes well, we create our own descendants and become somebody's ancestor. Kinship; that's what makes the world go round.

In our family of procreation we are promoted from child of our parents to parent of our children. Our parents become grandparents, considered by some to be a fringe benefit of being a parent in the first place.

Family of affinity

Obviously, the object of your affection didn't spring forth like Venus rising from the sea foam. The only foam you will see is the sputtering of your intended's parents if they don't think you're good enough for their darling. Along with your mate comes a ready-made bevy of relatives, and like it or not, you've acquired another family.

The family of your spouse is your family of affinity, and the members are your **in-laws**. Your beloved's parents are your **mother-in-law** and **father-in-law**. Spousal siblings are your **brothers-in-law** and **sisters-in-law**. Technically, the husband or wife of a brother-in-law or sister-in-law is not an in-law; however, as a courtesy they are introduced as such.

All blood relatives of your spouse become your **affinity relatives**, and by adding the term "in-law" or the phrase "**by marriage**," we instantly identify to the world their place in our kinship circle. Usually, the term in-law is eliminated when addressing aunts, uncles, grandparents, and cousins. Most people introduce affinity relatives as Aunt Jane or Uncle Toby, unless Aunt Jane has fallen into the punch bowl, or Uncle Toby has gone skinny-dipping in the fishpond. Then it's perfectly acceptable to announce quite distinctly, "My *husband's* Aunt Jane and Uncle Toby really do know how to have a good time."

A family of affinity is ours only so long as we remain married to our spouse. Unfortunately, due to death or divorce, affinity relationships are often severed. Only the rare family can look beyond the problems of a couple, remain neutral, and stay on good terms with both parties.

If you're ever in the unhappy situation of divorce, spare your children the pain of separation from the family of your ex-spouse. Remember, they may have been your family of affinity, but they are your children's family of orientation.

From our family of orientation we learn who we are and where we came from. In our family of procreation we pass along the genes and learned behavior of past generations and continue kinship connections; and from our family of affinity we learn patience, forbearance, and tolerance, hopefully. God bless 'em all.

5 • Family

I am the family face; Flesh perishes, I live on.
Thomas Hardy, Heredity

Family defined

The term "family" generally refers to parents and their children, and the term includes people related by blood, affinity, or adoption, whether or not they all live in the same house.

The meaning of family is more legally restrictive when relatives simply live together because it's convenient or economical. This is an especially important distinction when dealing with insurance and wills, and this distinction is carefully considered when one person is ordered to support another.

Legal obligations between spouses and their duties to their offspring take precedence over all others. However, your marital status isn't so exclusive that you must give up your family of orientation. For example: you can't legally prevent your spouse from visiting with kindred even if you personally can't stand them.

Family law

"Family law" refers to the body of law relating to marriage, divorce, adoption, paternity, and other familial relationships.

In the past, law schools tended to neglect the emotional impact on relatives when differences had to be settled in court.

It is greatly significant that a quarter of all murder victims in the United States are killed by kin—and that 50 percent of those murders are at the hands of a spouse. Attorneys are now looking for ways to reduce tensions between familial litigants before the shooting starts.

Although our laws favor the marital relationship and encourage the permanence of traditional families, courts today must address many new concepts, from palimony to prenuptial agreements, same-gender arrangements, surrogate parenting, and grandparents' rights.

Children

Children are protected by law from neglect or abuse and are entitled to the protection of the state. They may be removed from their parents' home if the state feels they are in danger. But, parents may use reasonable discipline when correcting their children.

Parents, whether married or divorced, must support their minor children, and the age when a child is considered an adult varies by state from 18 to 21 years of age. Once a child is "emancipated" (becomes an adult and leaves the parental home), there is no further parental responsibility. Emancipation for minors is possible if the parents agree and the child is self-supporting, and there is no legal responsibility for parents to continue support except in extremely mitigating circumstances.

All states regulate the ages of compulsory education for children. The age at which a child must be enrolled in school varies from 6 to 8 years, and the age at which a child may leave school varies from as young as 13 in Mississippi to as old as 18 in Hawaii, Ohio, Oklahoma, Oregon, Washington, and Wisconsin. But, after that parental obligation is met, further educational assistance is usually voluntary unless ordered in a divorce decree.

When the deliberate misdeeds of children result in financial losses to a third party, the parents are sometimes ordered to make restitution. And, parents can't disown a child under the age of 16. The best they can do to curb unruly progeny is to request court intervention.

Orphans, foster children, and foundlings

A child who has lost both parents, or sometimes a child who has lost one parent (especially a father), is considered an **orphan**. When children are orphaned, there is no obligation on the part of kindred to take them in.

To **foster** means to nurture, feed, or provide the love and protection that, for whatever reason, isn't forthcoming from natural parents. Fostering by choice is an age-old practice that shouldn't be confused with court-sanctioned custodial care for which the caretakers are compensated by society.

In ancient Ireland and in several other societies, particularly those of the Middle East, families frequently sent their offspring to a "fosterer." Sometimes the foster relationship became emotionally stronger than the original blood kinship.

Wet nurses (women who breast-feed children of other women) have historically played an important part in family life. At the time when the Prophet Mohammed was born, infants from wealthy homes were sent into the desert to be suckled and raised to adolescence. Unfortunately for little Mohammed, the more desirable nurses were looking for influential alliances and they scoffed at his background. Eventually, an undistinguished woman took pity and accepted Mohammed into her family. According to legend, she began to experience a multitude of heavenly blessings, which were interpreted as omens of the child's future greatness. No doubt the reluctant nurses regretted their own lack of foresight.

A **foundling** is a baby deserted by its parents. In ancient societies, and maybe a few modern ones, unwanted infants— especially girls—were abandoned to the elements much as some people dispose of excess cats and dogs. Anyone in the United States who abandons a child is subject to criminal prosecution.

Illegitimate children

If a man's wife has borne him sons, and his maidservant has borne him sons, (and) if the father in his lifetime has called the sons of the maidservant 'my sons,' (and) has numbered them with the sons of his wife...the sons of the wife and the sons of the maidservant shall share equally in the goods of the (deceased) father's house....
Code of Hammurabi

A child born to an unmarried woman is illegitimate (not legally acceptable) and is considered to be a bastard.

Although bastards have biological ties to a particular family, the law believes that nothing should interfere with cohesive, legal family structure and inheritance procedures. In order for a bastard to take his place in a paternal kinship group, an unmarried woman must present positive proof of her child's paternity, or the alleged father must admit responsibility.

Acceptance of illegitimate children ebbs and flows with the times. Bastards fared better in 15th-century France and Germany than at any other time in history. Most nobles and gentlemen provided their illegitimate sons with excellent educations and arranged good marriages for their illegitimate daughters.

In Europe, illegitimate children could be legitimized if the parents later married, although the English resisted the idea well into the 20th century, claiming once a bastard always a bastard. This thinking is now obsolete.

To **legitimize** means to put a bastard in the position, or state, of a legitimate child before the law, by legal means; legitimization must be distinguished from adoption, which has no reference to blood relation. Acceptance doesn't have to be spoken, but may be silent. Silence, when one is under a duty to speak, may be more effective than words. If a child is welcomed into the paternal family, this is considered public acknowledgment even if the father remains silent.

The basic difference between bastards and their legitimate siblings is that illegitimate offspring can't receive any portion of the paternal estate that isn't freely given during the lifetime of the father or specified in his will.

Adoption

If a man has taken a young child to sonship, and has reared him up, no one (else) has a claim against that nursling.

Code of Hammurabi

Adoption means that a person takes the child of another and, within the legal system, gives that child the rights, privileges, and responsibilities of one's biological offspring. The adopted individual assumes the same legal relationship as any legitimate child would have.

There are a few exceptions. Some clubs such as the Daughters of the American Revolution make "blood" a mandatory requirement for membership. These organizations recognize that anyone can be legally adopted with all attendant legal rights, but they argue that adoptees can't take on the heritage of the adopting family. Courts generally agree with them. Courts have also upheld the rights of persons to will ancestral estates to blood relatives to the exclusion of adoptees.

Although every state recognizes adoption, each has its own guidelines regarding what is in the best interests of the child and the age at which the child's consent is required. They also consider the age, marital status, occupation, financial status, character, race, and religion of the adopting adult. Some states require the adopting parents to be married and living together; others allow almost any qualified adult to adopt, although laws in Florida and New Hampshire prevent homosexuals from adopting.

The Uniform Adoption Act provides that adoption records must be sealed (unavailable for public scrutiny) and are subject to inspection only upon court order and usually with the consent of all interested parties. Currently the only states that permit adult adoptees to see their birth records are Alabama, Alaska, and Kansas. A few other states will open the files if the biological parent consents. In the 47 states where records are sealed, a new birth certificate is issued with the names of the adopting parents replacing those of the biological parents.

The National Committee for Adoption opposes opening sealed records, feeling that the privacy of birth mothers must be protected. Another agency, Adoption Identity Movement (AIM), counters with the argument that an adoptee has a greater right to know his heritage than his biological mother has to privacy.

Interestingly enough, in Alabama, Louisiana, Mississippi, Oklahoma, Rhode Island, South Dakota, Texas, Vermont, and Wyoming, adoptees retain inheritance rights from the natural parent if that parent dies without a will. In those states where adoption records remain sealed, how would adoptees ever learn they were potential heirs?

In the cases of artificial insemination, test-tube babies, and children born of surrogate mothers, the Uniform Status of Children of Assisted Conception Act follows the established adoption procedure of altering birth certificates. The Uniform Parentage Act doesn't require listing the names of the biological parents; i.e., the sperm and ovum donors.

Genealogists find the issuance of altered birth certificates appalling under any circumstances. At some time in the future, they say, adoptees (who constitute 2 percent of the American population) and the growing number of assisted-conception children will be deceived into tracing their lineage to people who are totally unrelated biologically. The legal rights of children born of assisted-conception methods are even more uncertain, although a recent sperm donor has sued to have visitation rights with the child born of his sperm.

Adult adoption

For the purposes of adoption, the term "child" doesn't necessarily mean a minor. In most states, an adult may adopt another adult who, in effect, becomes the "child" of the adopting person. The laws governing adult adoption aren't as stringent as those regarding the adoption of minors. Usually all that's required to adopt an adult is mutual consent and United States citizenship on the part of both parties. Some states require that the adopting person be at least 10 to 15 years older than the person being adopted. Alabama, Arizona, Hawaii, Michigan, Nebraska, and Ohio do not permit adult adoptions under any circumstances.

Adoption annulments

If a man has taken a young child to sonshlp, and... his (biological) father and mother rebelled, that nursling shall return to his father's house.
                                    Code of Hammurabi

Under special circumstances, adoptions may be revoked. The biological mother may change her mind and ask to have the child returned. A court may annul an adoption if the adoption was procured because of misrepresentation by the adopting parents, and adoptions may be revoked by the mutual consent of the parties involved. Adoptions can't be challenged after the death of either party.

Responsibilities to other relatives

Financial support

Many states have "poor laws" that require a person to support, in addition to a spouse and minor children, impoverished adult children, parents, grandparents, grandchildren, and siblings. If a family is able to help but refuses, and if the relative becomes a burden on the state, the family may be charged for the cost. The expense is usually prorated among kindred in the same degree of consanguinity to the indigent. In other states, a person has no legal obligation to anyone other than a spouse and minor children.

Bone marrow and Tissue transplants

Another area the courts are increasingly addressing is whether relatives can be forced to donate organs, bone marrow, or other tissue to ill family members. Because most transplants work best when the donor is biologically compatible with the recipient, individuals are turning to kindred for help. So far, the courts have refused to intervene even if it means the death of the person requesting the donation.

Recently, a Pennsylvania judge heard a case where a man had previously agreed to donate bone marrow to his cousin. After the cousin underwent radiation therapy in preparation for the operation, the relative refused to go through with the procedure. The cousin sued for breach of promise. Although the judge felt the relative's actions were despicable, he ruled that courts can't force anyone to undergo medical tests or procedures and that persons who have agreed to do so may change their minds. The cousin died within days of the ruling.

A Chicago man sued the unmarried mother of his infant twins when she refused to allow them to be tested to determine if they were medically compatible with his son by another woman. The man wanted the twins to provide bone marrow for the son, who suffered from leukemia. The court ruled against the plan.

On the other hand, it isn't illegal to conceive for the sole purpose of aborting the fetus for its tissue, or for the purpose of bearing a live child as a potential organ donor.

Abortion is the most common surgical procedure in the United States. Medical laboratories claim that the resulting fetal tissue might as well be used. The courts haven't yet addressed the issue, and theologians and others are raising questions about its moral implications.

In 1973, the United States Supreme Court ruled that an unborn child is the mother's property, to be dispensed with and disposed of as she sees fit. If a woman decides to conceive and abort a fetus and she then sells it for medical research, she does so legally at the present time. The father has no right to interfere with the mother's decision. The United States Supreme Court has recently reviewed the landmark decision in *Roe v. Wade* (the case that legalized abortion), and has made some changes in abortion laws, much to the dismay of pro-choice activists.

Frozen embryos

Cryopreservation, the freezing and storage of fertilized human eggs, is a technique that came into use several years ago. At the present time, clinics offering the service set their own rules. The federal government is studying ways to regulate the practice.

Many questions have been raised. Should parents be compelled to donate unused eggs to other couples? May parents dispose of extra embryos once they have had a child? Should a woman whose spouse has died be permitted to have a frozen embryo implanted? Would the resulting child be entitled to inheritance rights? Should frozen embryos be created for medical research purposes? Could parents donate frozen embryos to their other offspring without violating civil incest laws? If the parents of the embryos die, must the frozen embryos be destroyed, or may they be implanted in a surrogate mother?

Court battles between divorced couples over custody of the frozen embryos and who decides whether the embryos may be used are becoming increasingly common. A Tennessee couple had several fertilized eggs frozen prior to their divorce. The ex-wife sought custody of the embryos because, she said, she may want to be a mother someday. The ex-husband said he chose not to be the father of her children. In addressing this case, the court ruled that the ex-wife had no right to force a man to be a father against his will, and she was prevented from implanting the embryos in herself or donating them to anyone else.

Grandparents' rights

It has always been assumed that grandparents and grandchildren have a special bond. That bond is being tested as more families experience dissension, divorce, and remarriage. The so-called "bookend generations" are caught in the crossfire of the warring couple.

Traditionally, third parties such as grandparents, siblings, and other relatives have had no legal right to seek visitation with underage kindred.

Prior to 1965, courts refused to interfere with grandchild-grandparent visitation, claiming that parents controlled such matters. Since that time, every state, under pressure from grandparents' rights groups, has addressed the plight of those denied the right to see their grandchildren.

In 1985, Congress touched on the issue in a resolution urging that a uniform grandparent visitation statute be developed. Without such a statute, grandparents who win visitation rights in one state may lose those rights if the custodial parent moves to a state where such rights are not recognized.

Other states act only in specific family situations, such as divorce, legal separation, or death of a parent. In cases where the child lives in a so-called "intact" family in which the parents are still married, or where the child has been adopted by a stepparent, the courts are less likely to intervene.

The general rule regarding the biological grandparents is that all ties are severed after a child is adopted. However, Georgia, Mississippi, Oklahoma, Texas, and Nevada will consider the right of grandparents to see their grandchildren who've been adopted by others.

Idaho will generally grant visitation rights when a grandparent can prove that severance of the relationship would be harmful to the child. North Dakota considers grandparents' rights only if the exercise of such rights would not interfere with the parent-child relationship. Several states, including Alaska, California, Delaware, Maine, and Maryland are encouraging mediation services.

Although all 50 states have legislation allowing grandparents to petition for the right to see their grandchildren, the myriad requirements make it extremely difficult for grandparents to know and understand their rights.

Richard S. Victor, attorney and founder of Grandparents Rights Organization (GRO) says, "I am confident that good, factual information about grandparents' rights disputes will contribute to the formation of fair and appropriate laws. Laws that will serve entire families."

GRANDPARENTS' VISITATION RIGHTS

KEY:
1. Courts consider grandparents' visitation rights in cases of divorce, legal separation, or death of parent.
2. No specific laws dealing with grandparents' custody rights.
3. Allows grandparents, siblings, great-grandparents, other relatives, and some non-relatives to petition for visitation.
4. Additional circumstances under which grandparents can seek visitation.

STATE	1	2	3	4
Alabama	•	•		
Alaska	•	•	•	Mediation legislation pending.
Arizona	•	•	•	
Arkansas	•	•	•	
California	•	•	•	Mediation.
Colorado	•	•		In third party custody or when child placed in foster care.
Connecticut	•	•		
Delaware	•	•		Mediation.
Florida	•	•		
Georgia	•			Allows visitation when rights of one parent are terminated by court order.
Hawaii	•	•		
Illinois	•	•	•	May file anytime.
Indiana	•			
Idaho	•	•		
Iowa	•	•		Third party custody; child in foster care, or when grandparents have a substantial relationship with the child in an 'intact' family.
Kansas	•			
Kentucky	•	•		
Louisiana	•			Third party custody; child in foster care; death of one party of an unmarried couple.
Maine	•		•	Mediation; may also file in cases where child's parents were never married.
Maryland	•	•		Mediation.
Massachusetts	•	•		May also file in cases where child's parents were never married.
Michigan	•		•	Third party custody, or child in foster care.
Minnesota	•	•		
Mississippi	•			Allows visitation if the rights of one parent are terminated by court order; will consider rights of biological grandparents to see adopted grandchildren.
Montana	•			
Missouri	•			Allows visitation after adoption if the child's natural parent is deceased.
Nebraska	•			
Nevada	•		•	Allows visitation when both parents' rights are terminated; will consider rights of biological grandparents to see grandchildren who have been adopted.
New York	•			Third party custody, or when child in foster care.
New Hampshire	•	•		May also file in cases where child's parents were never married.
New Jersey	•	•	•	
New Mexico	•			
North Carolina	•			
North Dakota	•		•	Grants 'intact' family visitation if in best interests of the child.
Ohio	•			
Oklahoma	•		•	May file anytime; allows visitation when the rights of one parent are terminated by the court; will consider the rights of biological grandparents in the case of adoption.
Oregon	•			
Pennsylvania	•	•		
Rhode Island	•			
South Carolina	•			
South Dakota	•		•	May file anytime, also allows visitation following adoption.
Tennessee	•			Allows petitions for abuse, neglect, abandonment, third party custody, or child in foster care.
Texas	•			Allows petitions for visitation in cases of abuse, neglect, abandonment, juvenile delinquency, incompetence, or parental incarceration; allows visitation when the rights of one parent are terminated by court order; will consider the biological grandparents' right to see their grandchildren in case of adoption.
Virginia	•	•		
Utah	•	•	•	
Vermont	•	•		In addition, allows in cases of abuse, neglect, and abandonment.
Washington	•	•	•	
West Virginia	•	•		
Wisconsin	•	•	•	
Wyoming	•	•		

Grandparents resource list

**Grandparents Rights
  Organization (QRO)**
Richard S. Victor, Founder,
  Executive Director
555 S. Woodward, Suite 600
Birmingham, MI 48009
810-646-7191

**Grandparents/Grandchildren:
  The Vital Connection**
Dr. Arthur Kornhaber and
  Kenneth Woodward
Transaction Books
Rutgers University
New Brunswick, NJ 08903
201-932-2280

**The New American
  Grandparent**
Andrew J. Cherlin
  Harper and Row
10 East 53rd St.
New York, NY 10022
212-207-7000

Grandparents Magazine
Better Homes and Gardens
Meredith Corporation
1716 Locust St.
Des Moines, IA 50336

**The Foundation for
  Grandparenting**
Box 31
Lake Placid, NY 12946

**Between Parents and
  Grandparents**
Dr. Arthur Kornhaber Berkley
Publishing 200 Madison Ave.
New York, NY 10016

**Grandparents for Children's
  Rights**
Lee and Lucille Sumpter
5728 Bayonne Ave.
Haslett, MI 48840
517-339-8663

**The American Self-Help
  Clearinghouse**
St. Clares-Riverside Medical
  Center
Denville, NJ 07834
201-625-7101

**Grandparents Against
  Immorality and Neglect
  (GAIN)**
Betty Parbs
720 Kingstown Pl.
Shreveport, LA 71108
318-688-4246

**Grandparents Raising
  Grandchildren**
Barbara Kirkland
PO Box 104
Colleyville, TX 76034

Second Time Around Parents
Michele Daly
Family and Community Services
  of Delaware County
100 W. Front St.
Media, PA 19063
215-566-7540

**Grandchildren Visitation
  Disputes (a manual)**
American Bar Association
ABA Order Fulfillment
750 Lake Shore Dr.
Chicago, IL 60611
  ($19.95 plus $2.95 p&h)

Grandparenting in the 90's:
Everything You Wanted to
Know about Grandparenting
Groups in America
(A directory)
Grandparents Are Us
PO Box 418
Patton, CA 92369

Miscellaneous

Wrongful death suits

> *If a man has caused the loss of a gentleman's eye, his (own) eye... shall be lost.*
> *If he has shattered a gentleman's limb, his (own) limb shall be shattered.*
> *If he has caused a poor man to lose his eye or shattered a poor man's limb, he shall pay one mina of silver.*
>
> **Code of Hammurabi**

Under Anglo-Saxon and ancient Scottish laws, **wergild** or **wergelt**—similar to the Old English **bloodwite**—was the money paid to the king and the relatives of the injured party by the person who committed the injury. The compensation depended upon the loss suffered and the rank of the injured party.

In the United States, some courts practice a modern version of wergild by allowing certain family members to bring wrongful death suits against anyone who has killed a spouse, child, or parent. They may be awarded pecuniary (money) damages if they can prove they suffered a loss of services, income, or other benefits.

Living-together and same-sex couples aren't allowed to sue for wrongful death because they have no legal relationship to the injured person.

Court proceedings

Prospective jurors in criminal and civil cases may be prevented from serving on juries if they are related to the defendant, prosecutor, or the complainant and if that relationship is deemed close enough to cause the jurors to be biased.

The degree of kinship varies from state to state. For example, in Alabama, jurors may be challenged if they are within the ninth degree of consanguinity, or the fifth degree of affinity. Degrees are determined by starting with the person in question, counting up to the common ancestor, and then down to the prospective juror.

For example, under the Alabama law, a juror could be challenged if he were the defendant's third cousin once removed or second cousin three times removed because that places him within the ninth degree of kinship. (See figure 7—Chart of consanguinity.)

Whether it's legal in a criminal trial for spouses to testify against each other depends upon the circumstances of the case and the state in which the case is heard. Generally, courts won't force spouses to testify because of the intimate nature of marriage. However, the Supreme Court has ruled that spouses may voluntarily testify against each other without the consent of the other spouse.

* * *

Vital statistics

All states maintain repositories where individual vital records are kept. Every birth, death, marriage, and divorce is recorded in the locality where the event occurred, and certified copies are available by contacting the appropriate vital statistics office in a city, county, or other local office. The following addresses have been provided for your convenience.

In order to obtain copies of birth, death, marriage, and divorce certificates, you must contact the appropriate department in the state where the event occurred. Write or call to determine fees, which must be paid in advance.

You must provide the following information:

For birth or death records:
- Full name of person whose record is being requested
- Sex
- Parents' names, including mother's maiden name
- Month, date, and year of birth or death
- Place of birth or death (include dry or town, county, state, and name of hospital if known)
- Purpose for which copy is needed
- Relationship to person whose record is being requested

For marriage records:
- Full names of bride and groom
- Month, day, and year of marriage
- Place of marriage (city, town, county, and state)
- Purpose for which copy is needed
- Relationship to persons whose record is being requested

For divorce records:
- Full names of husband and wife
- Date of divorce or annulment
- Place of divorce or annulment
- Type of final decree
- Purpose for which copy is needed
- Relationship to persons whose record is being requested

Note: If you are a United States citizen who needs a copy of a foreign birth or death record, contact the Office of Overseas Citizens Foreign Services, U.S. Department of State, Washington, DC 20520.

ALABAMA
Center for Health Statistics
State Public Health Department
434 Monroe St
Montgomery, AL 36130-1701
205-242-5033

ALASKA
Vital Statistics Bureau
Rm. 115, Alaska Office Building
Pouch H-02Q
Juneau, AK 99811-0675
907-465-3391

ARIZONA
Vital Records Section
Department of Health Services
PO Box 3887
Phoenix, AZ 85030
602-542-1080

ARKANSAS
Division of Vital Records
Arkansas Department of Health
4815 West Markham
Little Rock, AR 72201
501-661-2336

CALIFORNIA
Vital Statistics Branch
Department of Health Services
410 N St.
Sacramento, CA 95814-4381
916-445-2684

COLORADO
Vital Records Section
Department of Health
4210 E. 11th Ave.
Denver, CO 80220
503-320-8474

CONNECTICUT
Vital Records Section
Division of Health Statistics
79 Elm St.
Hartford, CT 06115
203-566-2334

DELAWARE
Bureau of Vital Statistics
Division of Public Health
Department of Health &
   Social Services
Jesse S. Cooper Memorial Bldg.
Dover, DE 19901
302-736-4721

DISTRICT OF COLUMBIA
Vital Records Branch
Department of Human Services
615 Pennsylvania Ave., NW
Washington, DC 20004
202-727-9281

FLORIDA
Bureau of Vital Statistics
Department of Health &
   Rehabilitative Services
PO Box 210
Jacksonville, FL 32231
904-359-6900

GEORGIA
Vital Records Service
State Dept of Human Resources
47 Trinity Ave., SW
Atlanta, QA 30334
404-656-4900

HAWAII
Research and Statistics Office
State Department of Health
PO Box 3378
Honolulu, HA 96801
808-548-5819

IDAHO
Vital Statistics Unit
State Department of Health
   and Welfare
450 West State St.
Statehouse Mail
Boise, ID 83720
208-334-5988

ILLINOIS
Division of Vital Records
State Dept of Public Health
605 W. Jefferson St.
Springfield, 1L 62702-5079
217-782-6553

INDIANA
Vital Records Section
State Board of Health
1330 W. Michigan St.
Indianapolis, IN 46202-1964
317-633-0275

IOWA
Department of Public Health
Vital Records Section
Lucas Office Building
321 E. 12th St.
Des Moines, IA 50319
515-281-5871

KANSAS
Office of Vital Statistics
Dept of Health fie Environment
900 Jackson St.
Topeka, KS 66620-1290
913-296-1400

KENTUCKY
Office of Vital Statistics
Department of Health Services
275 E. Main St.
Frankfort, KY 40621
502-564-4212

LOUISIANA
Vital Records Registry
Office of Public Health
325 Loyola Ave.
New Orleans, LA 70112
207-289-3184

MAINE
Office of Vital Records
Human Services Building
Station 11, State House
Augusta, ME 04333
207-289-3184

MARYLAND
Division of Vital Records
Department of Health and
    Mental Hygiene
4201 Patterson Ave.
PO Box 68760
Baltimore, MD 21215-0020
410-225-5988

MASSACHUSETTS
Registry of Vital Records
    and Statistics
150 Tremont St., Rm B-3
Boston, MA 02111
617-727-7388

MICHIGAN
Office of the State Registrar
    Center for Health Statistics
Michigan Dept of Public Health
3423 North Logan St.
Lansing, MI 48909
517-335-8655

MINNESOTA
Minnesota Dept of Health
Section of Vital Statistics
717 Delaware St., SE
PO Box 9441
Minneapolis, MN 55440
612-623-5121

MISSISSIPPI
Vital Records
State Department of Health
2423 North State St.
Jackson, MS 39216
601-960-7981,601-960-7450

MISSOURI
Department of Health
Bureau of Vital Records
1730 East Elm
PO Box 570
Jefferson City, MO 65102
314-751-6387 (Birth)
314-751-6376 (Death)

MONTANA
Bureau of Records and Statistics
State Department of Health and
    Environmental Sciences
Helena, MT 59620
406-444-2614

NEBRASKA
Bureau of Vital Statistics State
Department of Health
301 Centennial Mall South
PO Box 95007
Lincoln, NE 68509-5007
402-471-2871

NEVADA
Division of Health-Vital Statistics
Capitol Complex
505 East King St., #102
Carson City,MV 89710
702-885-4480

NEW HAMPSHIRE
Bureau of Vital Records
Health and Human Services
    Building
6 Hazen Dr.
Concord, MH 03301
603-271-4654

NEW JERSEY
State Department of Health
Bureau of Vital Statistics
South Warren and Market St.
CN 370
Trenton, NJ 87503
609-292-4087

NEW MEXICO
Vital Statistics
New Mexico Health Services Div.
1190 St Francis Dr.
Santa Fe, NM 87503
505-827-2338

NEW YORK
Vital Records Section
State Department of Health
Empire State Plaza
Tower Building
Albany, NY 12237-0023
518-474-3075

NEW YORK CITY
Bureau of Vital Records
Department of Health of
New York City 125 Worth St.
New York, MY 10013
212-619-4530

NORTH CAROLINA
Dept of Environment Health,
    and Natural Resources
Division of Epidemiology
Vital Records Section
225 M. McDowell St.
PO Box 27687
Raleigh, MC 27611-7687
919-733-3526

NORTH DAKOTA
Division of Vital Records
State Capitol
600 E. Boulevard Ave.
Bismarck, MD 58505
701-224-2360

OHIO
Division of Vital Statistics
Ohio Department of Health
G-20 Ohio Department Building
65 S. Front St.
Columbus, OH 43266-0333
614-466-2531

OKLAHOMA
Vital Records Section
State Department of Health
1000 Mortheast 10th St.
PO Box 53551
Oklahoma City, OK 73152
405-271-4040

OREGON
Oregon Health Division
Vital Statistics Section
PO Box 116
Portland, OR 97207
503-229-5710

PENNSYLVANIA
Division of Vital Records
State Department of Health
Central Building
101S. Mercer St
PO Box 1528
New Castle, PA 16103
412-656-3147

RHODE ISLAND
Division of Vital Records
Rhode Island Dept of Health
Room 101, Cannon Building
3 Capitol Hill
Providence, RI 02908-5079
401-277-2811

SOUTH CAROLINA
Office of Vital Records
   and Public Health Statistics
South Carolina Dept of Health
   and Environmental Control
2600 Bull St.
Columbia, SC 29201
803-734-4830

SOUTH DAKOTA
State Department of Health
Center for Health Policy
   and Statistics
Vital Records
523 E. Capitol
Pierre, SD 57501
605-773-3355

TENNESSEE
Tennessee Vital Records
Department of Health and
   Environment
Cordell Hull Building
Nashville, TN 37219-5402
615-741-1763
800-423-1901 (Tennessee
   residents)

TEXAS
Bureau of Vital Statistics
Texas Department of Health
1100 W. 49th St.
Austin, TX 78756-3191
512-458-7451

UTAH
Bureau of Vital Records
Utah Department of Health
288 N. 1460 West
PO Box 16700
Salt Lake City, UT 84116-0700
801-538-6105

VERMONT
Vermont Department of Health
Vital Records Section
Box 70
60 Main St
Burlington, VT 05402
802-863-7275

VIRGINIA
Division of Vital Records
State Health Department
PO Box 1000
Richmond, VA 23208-1000
804-786-6228

WASHINGTON
Vital Records
1112 South Quince
PO Box 9709, ET-11
Olympia, WA 98505-9709
206-753-5936
800-551-0562 (out of state)
800-331-0680 (state residents)

WEST VIRGINIA
Vital Registration Office
Division of Health
State Capitol Complex Bldg. 3
Charleston, WV 25305
304-348-2931

WISCONSIN
Vital Records
1 West Wilson St.
PO Box 309
Madison, WI 53701
608-266-1371

WYOMING
Vital Records Services
Hathaway Building
Cheyenne, WY 82002
307-777-7591

This information has been supplied by the National Center for Health Statistics, U.S. Department of Health and Human Services, Public Health Service, Hyattsville, MD, DHHS Publication No. (PHS) 90-1142.

6 • Names

*I would to God thou and I knew where a commodity
of good names were to be bought.*

Henry IV, Shakespeare

In *Romeo and Juliet*, Shakespeare speaks through a character, "What's in a name? that which we call a rose, By any other name would smell as sweet." That's a wonderful sentiment but, according to some psychologists, not exactly accurate. Studies have shown that teachers often subconsciously favor children with "pretty" or "traditional" first names. Students with offbeat or eccentric names are not called upon as often as those with more acceptable names, and their written work is judged more harshly than that of their traditionally named classmates.

Although parents have comparative freedom when choosing a first name for their child, tradition dictates that children take the last names or surnames (from the French surnom) of their fathers. Males generally retain their birth names all of their lives, while females have tended to use their fathers' last names until they marry—then they take the surnames of their husbands. But, this is merely tradition, not law, and the tradition has begun to change.

As more people become aware of their right to choose their names and as women's rights groups urge women to retain their birth names, couples sometimes elect to use both names, either with or without a hyphen. A small minority are inventing names, and a few even choose different last names for each child. Genealogists say the thought of such diversity is driving them crazy. They claim that charting family trees will become almost impossible if the trend continues.

Surnames of married women

Many people hold the erroneous belief that a woman *must* take her husband's last name when she marries. This belief is based upon the English tradition that required a woman to assume her husband's family name.

In the past, American courts followed that tradition and tended to deny a married woman the common-law right to use whatever name she chose. This is no longer the case— although in some states, a woman who wishes to retain her birth name may have to press her case rather diligently.

Although most women still adopt their spouses' names, many opt to retain their fathers' names for business or personal reasons, to avoid the hassle of changing countless identification papers, and to maintain a continuous identity throughout their lives.

Passports are a different matter. From 1925 to 1966, a married woman had a problem using her birth name on her passport. Witnesses were required to swear that the woman had used her maiden name exclusively for a stated period of time. After 1966, a new regulation took effect that required an applicant whose name had been changed by court order to submit a certified copy of the decree. Any applicant whose name change was adopted without court proceedings had to show evidence that the name had been publicly and exclusively used over a long period of time.

Women already established in their spouses' names, and who then resume the use of their birth names without court sanction, must carry a passport listing both names for ten years. Brides who change their name to that of their husbands and divorcees who resume the use of a former name are issued passports using only one name. No proof of marriage or divorce is required. The Passport Office requires proof of a married woman's identity only when she uses her maiden name. Even today, a married woman may have difficulty getting a passport in her birth name. Her success depends upon the clerk with whom she deals, her legal knowledge, and her willingness to pursue the matter.

Surnames of children

The surnames of children fall into a gray area. Legally, an unmarried mother may give her child any surname she pleases, although bureaucrats may try to force her to give the child her birth name. Whether a child born to a married woman must take his or her father's name is also uncertain. When the courts are asked to decide the question, they usually rule that the father furnishes his child's surname and that his permission is needed for a name change.

A child over the age of 7 is sometimes consulted if there is conflict between the parents over the child's name. Under the age of 7 but over the age of 4, courts almost always favor the traditional preference for the paternal name. If there are compelling reasons for changing the name of an infant, the courts tend to be more sympathetic to the custodial parent, reasoning that an infant hasn't bonded with any name at that point and won't suffer psychological damage if the name were changed.

Hawaii, North Carolina, Florida, Louisiana, New Hampshire, and other states with restrictive naming laws are increasingly coming under attack by civil rights organizations. Some courts have gone on record as stating that restrictive naming laws "impinge upon decisions affecting family life, procreation, and child rearing; areas of human experience which the Supreme Court has long held must be accorded special protection."

First names

In the United States, parents have total freedom when choosing first names for their children, although courts would probably not allow registration of any name commonly considered vulgar or obscene.

Other countries are not so lenient. In 1803, Napoleon officially forbade offbeat first names, and only recently have French magistrates begun to allow unusual names. Even now, the parents must prove that a name is accepted and used regularly in other parts of the world.

Name changes

If you can't please everybody, then you might as well please yourself. That's why our laws allow people to change their names for whatever reason as long as there is no intent to defraud. If, after careful consideration, you feel you'd be happier if your name were easier to spell and pronounce, or if your name causes titters of amusement, then by all means, change it.

Every state has a fairly simple change of name law. There are some practical details, such as requesting the precise forms, knowing how to set up a legal notice of intent, and determining which day the case is scheduled before the court. Court clerks can explain the procedure. An attorney usually isn't necessary. A name can be changed in whole or in part. If a person is married, the spouse might have to join in the petition. A court appearance is required, at which a magistrate usually asks a few questions and then grants the request.

In most states, anyone can make a common-law name change simply by using the new name on a regular and consistent basis and notifying creditors, banks, insurance companies, and others who should know. However, under the Social Security system and other highly regulated areas of life, one is required to follow legal procedure in order to effect a name change. Additional information can be obtained from your local Bureau of Records or its equivalent.

For an in-depth look at name origins, how names are chosen, how they are used, naming patterns, and names and the occult, you might want to read *What's In A Name* by Leonard R.N. Ashley (published by Genealogical Publishing Company, Inc.).

7 • Wills

A Grave Undertaking

If a man has apportioned to his son, the first in his eyes . . . has written him a sealed deed, after the father has (died), when the brothers divide, the present his father gave him he shall take, and over and above he shall share equally in the goods of his father's house.

                                        The Code of Hammurabi

Distribution of wealth after death hasn't always been regulated by society. A family's retention of a deceased member's property often depended upon the ages of the deceased's children and the strength of his kindred. Primitive man may have hoped his sons would retain his stone ax, bearskin, or tiger tooth, but in reality his spouse(s), children, and belongings were vulnerable to any stronger individual or family group.

The right to inherit is a concept that has evolved over thousands of years and was not always based on kinship to the parents, nor was it a right enjoyed by everyone. During the Dark Ages, ordinary people couldn't make wills at all. The Greeks were the first to consider the rights of children to inherit from a parent. In more primitive times, inheritance was determined by the mother's line but, under patriarchy, inheritance began to be determined through the father's lineage.

During the 12th century, male inheritance rights were believed to be superior to those of the female. The rights of an heiress could be set aside in favor of a male relative. If a man died leaving only female issue, his fortune went to his closest male relative, no matter how distantly related, whether lineal or collateral.

Anglo-Saxons, influenced by the Romans, had quickly understood the notion that if an estate were divided among too many family members, there soon wouldn't be anything of consequence left, so they continued the **rule of primogeniture**, whereby the eldest male descendant became heir to the entire family fortune.

Primogeniture was abolished in the United States shortly after the Revolution, but in England, the practice has historically determined not only inheritance of property but of titles as well. Margaret Thatcher's family is a classic example. As a former prime minister of Great Britain, Mrs. Thatcher is entitled to a hereditary earldom. Upon her death, the title passes to her son, Mark. Mark is two minutes older than his twin sister, Carol. If Mark should die, the title passes to his son. Even if Mark had no son, the title would not go to Carol or any of her descendants. According to John Brooke-Little of the College of Arms, "The rule of primogeniture is enshrined in the law. To change that would open a can of worms. It would open up a lot of other cases."

Ultimogeniture was a little-used practice whereby whatever remained after the parents' death went to the youngest male, under the assumption that he would be the least established. Obviously, older siblings didn't care for that. Unfortunately, orphans have historically had to rely on the honesty of their guardians. Maternal uncles appear to have been more protective than paternal uncles and less likely to plunder estates of orphans—possibly because under the patriarchal system, the mother's side had less to gain.

will, n.: *wish; desire; pleasure; inclination; choice. A written instrument executed with the formalities of law, whereby a person makes a disposition of his property to take place after his death.*

testament, n.: *a disposition of personal property to take place after the owner's demise.*
Black's Law Dictionary

In the United States, courts prefer that you make provision for distribution of your worldly goods by writing a will. A will is a legal document that, in effect, says that while you can't take it with you, you can have a say about what's done with it after you're gone.

Legally, when a person expresses his wish that a certain disposition be made of his real and personal property after his death, the word "will" becomes a legal command. Will and testament have become synonymous in common usage.

A will is valid if made while the person (a male is called a "testator" and a female is called a "testatrix") making the will is lucid and without pressure from anyone, and if the document is executed properly in the presence of at least two witnesses. Some states require the witnesses to sign in the presence of each other and the testator or testatrix, but others require only that witnesses sign in the will maker's presence. A witness can not benefit from the provisions of the will.

Wills should be reviewed annually to see if there has been a change in any of the circumstances on which the will was based, especially in the event of marriage. In some states, marriage nullifies existing wills, because a spouse has a legal right to a certain share of the estate that can't be governed by will.

A remaining female spouse becomes a widow or dowager, and a surviving male spouse becomes a widower. Historically, a widow's share of her deceased husband's estate was called "dower" and a widower's share of his deceased wife's estate was called "curtesy." Dower and curtesy are now commonly known as the **statutory share**—the amount allowed by statute— and the amount differs by state. If a decedent has attempted to will all money away from a spouse, the spouse may elect to take the statutory amount.

In some states, the person making the will may disinherit adult children (e.g., "I decree that my rotten kid, John, receive nothing and he knows why!"); however, if a legitimate child isn't mentioned at all (called a pretermitted heir) in a will, the courts may assume the omission was an oversight and assign a legally acceptable amount to that child. In Kansas, Wyoming, and the District of Columbia, there are no rules governing pretermitted heirs. But, in Louisiana, which retains the French **legitime**, legitimate offspring are entitled by law to share in the parental estate and cannot be denied this right by will. In Connecticut, Georgia, and Indiana, the birth of a child revokes a prior will.

If a testator wants a grandchild to inherit, the child must be specifically named in the will. Grandchildren have no automatic inheritance rights, although they may sometimes receive a share by right of representation through a deceased parent.

While most states (check with the authorities in your state) honor wills written entirely in the handwriting of the testator (holographic or olographic will), the courts are meticulous in making sure there is compliance with the precise terms of that state's particular statutory definition and requirements of holographic wills. In some states, a holographic will must be witnessed and in others, not. Some states will void a holographic will if any printed material is found on the will. Some interpretations are so strict that even a stamped date will void the otherwise handwritten will.

Oral wills made by dying persons in the presence of witnesses and later reduced to writing (nuncupative wills) have been accepted, but aren't recognized in all states. In cases where they have been accepted, competent witnesses must swear to the oral wishes of the deceased. Again, as in other more conventional wills, the witnesses can't share in the estate. We can't have someone claiming, "Yep, just before Nellie croaked, she looked me straight in the eye and said she wanted me to have it all."

If a handwritten or oral will isn't your style, but you still hesitate to contact a lawyer, consider will forms, which are generally straightforward, short, and often free. (Michigan has recently made available a "statutory will kit." Contact your state senator or representative to find out if your state has something similar.)

However, in today's complicated society, everyone is advised to consult a skilled professional if they have considerable assets or complicated legal questions.

No matter how or by whom the document is drawn, it must contain no items that are illegal, repugnant, or shocking to society's conscience. Having said that, we can say that almost anything else goes. Then again, no matter how carefully a will is written, disgruntled wannabe heirs can challenge its validity. A court may revoke or amend a will if there is a very good legal reason—such as incompetence of the testator, fraud, or undue influence.

Where there's a will, there's a relative. On the other hand, when there is no will, there is also a relative and the state and a lawyer and a friend and. . . . Well, you get the idea.

And, when an intestate estate (one without a will) is being settled, people who haven't ever given genealogy a thought suddenly develop an intense interest in how closely related they were to dear, departed Nellie.

There are four basic ways by which courts dispose of Nellie's estate when there is no will: the **parentelic system**; the **degree of relationship system**; the **canon law system**; and the **Uniform Probate Code**.

Under the parentelic system, the law first looks to Nellie's issue (children, grandchildren, and any great-grands). If none exist, they look to her siblings, and then to nieces and nephews. If there are no siblings, the law looks for Nellie's aunts, uncles, and cousins. If unsuccessful, the search turns to grandparents, grandaunts, and granduncles. In the unlikely event that they again come up empty-handed, the law looks for great-grandparents. There is a problem at this point, because the law informally considers such distant relatives as **tangential** (touching lightly), or laughing heirs. Laughing heirs are those relatives so distant they didn't seek out Nellie when she was alive, didn't know she was dead, and wouldn't have cared if they had known—unless they heard about some money. That's when they start laughing—and scrambling for a perch on her family tree.

Using the degree of relationship system (see figure 7, Chart of consanguinity), one can produce a chart that shows relationships by degrees, the degrees being indicated by a series of numbered steps. The closer the degree of kinship to the decedent (designated "0"), the greater the claim (i.e., the lower the number of the degree, the greater the kinship and the claim). All persons of the same degree share equally.

Under the canon or common law system, the count goes up to the nearest common ancestor, then down to the relative in question. Thus, for example, first cousins are related in the fourth degree.

The Uniform Probate Code (UPC) is a limited version of the parentelic system, again looking first to the spouse and issue, then to parents, issue of parents, grandparents and their issue, and finally to the state. The UPC never goes beyond issue of grandparents; thus it avoids the laughing-heir problem.

Once the legal heirs are determined, the court decides the amount each person is entitled to receive. Shares may be divided by either the **per stirpes** or the **per capita** method.

Per stirpes (by representation of a deceased ancestor) is the system whereby a person takes the share to which their ancestor, if living, would have been entitled. For example: Nellie has three children, two surviving offspring and one who preceded her in death. Under the per stirpes method, Nellie's estate would be divided into three equal shares. Each surviving child would receive one share, with the deceased sibling's share going to his heirs.

By the per capita method, all heirs of equal degree share without reference to their right of representation. Under the per capita method, Nellie's estate would be divided into two shares; one portion for each surviving child. Children of the deceased sibling would receive nothing—and probably wouldn't ever speak to their aunt and uncle again.

There are some interesting exceptions to the methods of distribution previously described. Children conceived prior to the decedent's death but born afterward inherit as if they had been born during the decedent's lifetime.

Illegitimate children inherit from the mother, but generally inherit from the father only if certain conditions are met:

1. **If the father subsequently marries the mother.**

2. **If the father has openly acknowledged and supported the child.**

3. **If paternity is established by the courts before the father's death.**

4. **If, after the father's death, the child offers clear and convincing proof.**

Half blood relatives generally take the same share as whole-blood relatives. There is no legal obligation to provide for stepchildren. Adopted children always inherit from adoptive parents, but the big question is whether they may inherit from the biological parents and their kinship group. States differ in this regard.

Collaterals and affines (in-laws) have no automatic inheritance rights. Spouses of blood relatives (siblings-in-law, etc.) inherit nothing unless specifically willed to them by the testator.

If there are no living relatives, the assets escheat (revert to the state) without further ado. Even when there are relatives, the state often tries to grab a portion. The state reasons that if you didn't care who got your money, it may as well take some too.

With the complications inherent in not making a will, you'd think that sensible people would hie themselves to the nearest attorney, but, unfortunately, only 10 percent of Americans execute a will. Do you really want the state to decide what's to be done with your money? Think about it.

8 • Kinship and Your Health

Know thyself.
Inscription over the entrance of the
Temple of Apollo at Delphi

Inheritance is generally thought of as money or property which parents, relatives, or friends have distributed in the past, or possibly will leave in the future. Laws of inheritance are concerned with an orderly transfer of wealth between persons and from one generation to the next, but there is another bequest over which the courts, as yet, have no control. This comes as a gift we can't reject any more than an offer from the "Godfather" could be refused. Kinship plays a major role. Part of every ancestor is being repeated in some measure in each tiny fetus.

Your genetic inheritance

In many ways, receiving good **genes** is more important than inheriting stocks and bonds. All of us know people, or whole families, who seem to defy the laws of common sense when it comes to abusing their bodies, and they get away with it. Other individuals exercise, follow nutritious diets, maintain proper weight levels, neither smoke nor drink, and still contract some life-threatening ailment. Why?

The Oracle of the Chicken Gizzard was approached by a young man seeking the secret of a long and healthy life. The Oracle consulted the stars and tossed bones on the ground. She tested wind direction and gazed into a crystal ball. She brewed countless cups of strong coffee and swirled the grounds. She ate seven deep-fried chicken gizzards and meditated. She counted the letters in his name and reduced them to a single digit. She read his palm, searching the faint, squiggly lines for clues. She consulted tarot cards and rune stones. When she was at last exhausted by her efforts, she leaned forward; the young man held his breath.

She spoke.

"Choose your ancestors well."

Researching genetic disease

Until very recently "choose the correct ancestors" was the best advice medical science could give. Researchers are now looking for large, extended families in which certain illnesses are prevalent. By studying the healthy members and comparing them to members who have already developed a particular disease, scientists hope to predict medical trends.

- University of Utah scientists studied colon cancer by utilizing ancestral records of the Church of Jesus Christ of Latter-day Saints (Mormon Church). Comparing these genealogical histories with a statewide tumor registry, they discovered a family with almost 10,000 members whose colon cancer rate was unusually high. Through extensive testing along kinship lines, scientists found a gene which causes a predisposition to this cancer.
- Manic depression strikes regularly in certain Amish clans. Janice Egeland, a medical sociologist, hopes to isolate and compare the suspect gene with other family groups that either maintain extensive family records or have members with good memories. Researchers will then try to predict which members might become afflicted.
- People with West African heritage are particularly concerned with sickle cell anemia. This is a form of inherited chronic anemia, found mainly amongst those with West African ancestry, in which many of the red blood cells become sickle-shaped.

In the very near future, a fertilized egg only a few hours old may be tested for undesirable genes. If a problem is discovered, the ovum may be destroyed, depending upon the wishes of the parents.

Countless couples are already trying to ensure the conception of the physically and mentally perfect child, including choosing the child's sex. Recently, two Japanese professors developed a technique which guarantees the birth of females in families who have histories of male-related type diseases. In ordinary circumstances, male babies are socially preferred over female babies.

Results and problems

If genetic testing had been possible in 1864, would that glorious artist, Toulouse-Lautrec, have been aborted?

Henri Marie Raymond de Toulouse-Lautrec was born into a proud, ruling-class family with an unbroken line descending from father to son since the year 1196. Toulouse-Lautrec's parents were first cousins, and their only surviving son suffered from dwarfism. The couple blamed their familial relationship for their son's condition and they may have been right.

Modern medical studies conclude that Toulouse-Lautrec suffered a rare form of dwarfism (pyknodysostosis) which is more common in offspring of consanguineous (closely related) parents. Henri suffered abnormally short limbs; his features coarsened, his lips thickened, he drooled uncontrollably, and his nose dripped constantly. He became bitter, cynical, and alcoholic. Genetic testing prior to his birth could have alerted his parents, making one wonder what their choice might have been.

In the search for the perfect child, what will happen to the damaged zygotes, those unfortunate, fertilized eggs found to be defective? Will they be given a decent burial with grieving relatives at the grave site, or will they be thrown out with yesterday's garbage? Will their existence be recorded in a family history, or will they be used for experimentation? Who will speak for unborn Toulouse-Lautrecs, dwarfed, ugly, talented little creatures, or the idiot savants whose mental functions are severely limited except for that one special, exceptional talent? Through no fault of their own, they are victims of a tangled kinship web.

Genes and your personality

Behavioral patterns are also being carefully scrutinized. "Nature versus nurture" has been debated for centuries, but only now are controlled scientific experiments directing attention toward inherited tendencies of aggression and passivity. Perhaps a combination of nature and nuture is needed to cause problems to surface.

Close examination of adoptees is yielding information that points to the gene theory of inherited predisposition to behavior traits. One theory suggests that if a predisposition for criminal activity exists in the genes, then certain stimuli might exacerbate the tendency into a full-fledged problem.

Researchers at the Minnesota Center for Twin and Adoption Research say some personality traits are at least partly determined by heredity in addition to environment. Psychologists compared personality test results for identical twins to those for the general population and calculated the average contribution of genes to the following traits:

Trait	Contribution of genes (percent)
Extroversion	61
Conformity	60
Creativity	55
Paranoia	55
Worry	55
Optimism	54
Aggressiveness	48
Ambitiousness	46
Orderliness	43
Intimacy	33

- By an amazing coincidence, Billy the Kid, Wild Bill Hickok, the Dalton Brothers, the Younger Brothers, and Frank and Jesse James were all blue-eyed blonds. Scientists would certainly collect a wealth of information if they could examine those men to ascertain if the same gene that made the blue eyes and blond hair contributed to their aggressive and adventurous natures.
- The Tarahumare Indians of the Sierra Madres in Mexico never commit crimes. Scientists might feel they have inherited a gene with a predisposition for passivity, whereas sociologists probably think it's because the Tarahumare don't spank their children.

A cynical grandmother was asked the difference between heredity, environment, and kinship. She quipped, "If the baby looks like his father, that's heredity. If he looks like a neighbor, that's environment. If he's accepted by the family, that's kinship."

AI, in vitro, and surrogacy

Until recently, an infertile woman who desired a child had two choices: adjust to her barren state, or adopt. If she chose adoption, she had to accept the fact that the child would be the genetic product of two other people. The child would not be an actual link in her kinship chain.

Presently, a woman with an infertile husband can be **artificially inseminated** with another man's sperm—AI. Since the law considers the child of a married woman to be her husband's responsibility, there is no basic legal conflict.

What happens if both husband and wife are infertile? An embryo is created in a test tube using donated ovum and sperm (**in vitro fertilization**). The resulting fertilized egg is implanted in the wife's womb, and if all goes well, she will bear a child.

But wait! What happens if she couldn't carry a child to term, or if her uterus had been surgically removed? The woman could have her ovum collected, fertilized with her husband's sperm (or that of a donor), and placed in the womb of another woman—a **surrogate mother**. When the gestation period is complete, a healthy baby is born and turned over to the couple contracting for the service. Everyone ignores the worn, tangled skein of kinship and lives happily ever after. Or do they?

Ethical problems

How many people are involved in creating this child? The husband and wife, the sperm donor, the ovum donor, and the woman from rent-a-womb—references supplied. We won't even count the scientists, doctors, technicians, and lawyers who were necessary. Perhaps they can best be compared to the matchmakers of olden days.

Who are the real parents of this baby?

What would happen if just one person in this group reconsidered? Do the parents of the sperm donor have any rights to know and love their grandchild? Must they ignore the pull of their blood? Will the donor of the egg mourn the loss of her child? Will the biological mother who has carried the child for nine months feel guilt and grief when the child is placed in another woman's arms?

If a child conceived through surrogate parenting, in vitro fertilization, or artificial insemination ever wishes to have a meeting with his sperm father, his ovum mother, or his family of orientation, will the courts order this information revealed in all circumstances, or only when there is proof of medical necessity, or not at all?

What happens if the child is defective? Must the contracting party accept damaged goods? Should there be a "lemon law" for newborn babies?

Noel Keane, a pioneer in surrogate law, requested a legal opinion to determine, in advance of a child's birth, the legal right of a couple to receive the child without resorting to adoption. In a landmark ruling, the judge ruled, subject to genetic testing, that the biological parents were the couple who had contributed the sperm and egg. This was the nation's first legal opinion in determining the parentage of a child conceived using in vitro fertilization in the womb of a surrogate mother. The interim order didn't become final until after the birth of a baby girl. During the interval, the child was legally parentless and without kindred.

Questions of ethics must be quickly resolved. We may eventually have a situation in which the contracting couple perishes together in an accident. The courts must decide if the child born posthumously to a surrogate mother is their legal heir. Who is responsible if it is determined that the child is not the genetic product of the couple? Can a surrogate be forced to raise a child when the contractors die before the contract is fulfilled? As Hardy, of Laurel and Hardy, would say, "It's a fine mess you've gotten us into!"

Medical charts

Until science perfects its techniques, we'll continue to play "gene roulette" unless we help ourselves by noting trends toward particular illnesses within our families. We can't wait for a research team to show up on our doorstep.

It's extremely important for families to compile a medical history. How often have you or a member of your family gone to the doctor and faced questions regarding personal or family health? Could you answer the queries?

If your family doesn't have a detailed medical history, why not appoint yourself medical historian? Become a kinologist!

The best way to begin is to compile a medical family tree. You will be concerned with blood relatives only. Talk with or write to relatives asking them to supply medical information about themselves and members of their families. There are charts you can use as examples at the end of this book.

Charts should also include any tendency toward substance abuse. Medical experts believe the proclivity for alcohol and drug abuse may be inherited.

Don't forget to include information about the family's mental health. Was a great-grandmother emotionally unstable? Is there a family history of Alzheimer's disease? If any family member committed suicide, make a note of it. In the event another relative begins to act in an unusual way, the knowledge might help you take action.

How did family members interact? Was the family situation fairly serene, or broken with conflict? Were any family members compulsively neat and clean, or the opposite, always slovenly and lazy, making everyone around them uncomfortable? Were most of the relatives middle of the road and moderate in their total behavior?

Was Aunt Zelda's drinking called the "vapors," and did the family ignore it, indicating a reluctance to face and deal with an unpleasant situation? Was an erratic and irrational relative allowed to disrupt the serenity of the family time after time without restraint? Continual refusal to deal with reality is an indication of the collective mental health of a family.

Don't worry about hurt feelings. After all, you don't plan to publish this information for the world to see. Your only purpose is to provide useful information to future generations.

Your family is made up of the good, the bad, the ugly, and the beautiful, so don't overlook the "good stuff." Allow space in your charts for talents.

If you record accomplishments without critical analysis, later generations will be warmed by the knowledge that a special talent, vocation, or avocation is shared with an ancestor. Learning that a long-departed relative had a particular talent may spur a great-grandchild to develop a latent talent of his own. Who knows what future genius is waiting for such inspiration?

By combining careful mate selection with genetic counseling (when indicated), and armed with a knowledge of family medical history, no one need play "gene roulette" with the lives of future kindred.

Medical Charts

Use these charts as guides. Add more space if needed, and other relevant details.

Children

Name_____   Name_____   Name_____

Born_____   Born_____   Born_____

Died_____   Died_____   Died_____

Cause of death:

_____   _____   _____

Other health problems:

_____   _____   _____

Relatives' special talents:

_____

_____

_____

Siblings

Name_____   Name_____   Name_____

Born_____   Born_____   Born_____

Died_____   Died_____   Died_____

Cause of death:

_____   _____   _____

Other health problems:

_____   _____   _____

Self and Spouse

Name_____   Name_____   Name_____

Born_____   Born_____   Born_____

Died_____   Died_____   Died_____

Cause of death:

_____   _____   _____

Other health problems:

_____   _____   _____

_____   _____   _____

Parents

Name_____   Name_____   Name_____

Born_____   Born_____   Born_____

Died_____   Died_____   Died_____

Cause of death:

_____   _____   _____

Other health problems:

_____   _____   _____

_____   _____   _____

Grandparents

Name_____ Name_____ Name_____ Name_____

Born _____ Born _____ Born _____ Born _____

Died _____ Died _____ Died _____ Died _____

Cause of death:

_____ _____   _____ _____

Other health problems:

_____ _____   _____ _____

_____ _____   _____ _____

Great-Grandparents

Name_____ Name_____ Name_____Name_____

Born _____Born _____ Born _____ Born _____

Died _____Died _____ Died _____ Died _____

Cause of death:

_____ _____ _____ _____

Other health problems:

_____ _____ _____ _____

_____ _____ _____ _____

Name_____ Name_____ Name_____Name_____

Born _____Born _____ Born _____ Born _____

Died _____Died _____ Died _____ Died _____

Cause of death:

_____ _____ _____ _____

Other health problems:

_____ _____ _____ _____

_____ _____ _____ _____

You will be fortunate if you can list your eight great-grandparents.

9 • Tracing Your Family Tree

Learn of your genealogical tree as much as is needed for the practice of active love toward blood relatives.

The Prophet Mohammed

Any significant social mobility creates renewed interest in genealogy, whether families move from country to city or simply up the social ladder. Families wonder who they are and where they came from.

There are several reasons to want to know our forebears: the personal rewards (it strengthens kinship ties), a sense of security (isn't it nice to know we belong), and a sense of pride (don't let the family down).

In the past ten years, **horizontal** (or **parallel**) **genealogy** has become the vogue. Experts study overlapping pedigrees to show that we are all members of the largest kinship group in existence—the family of man. Horizontal genealogy creates some strange bedfellows. For instance, Jimmy Carter and Richard Nixon are sixth cousins, while Richard Nixon and George Bush are tenth cousins once removed. Wouldn't that make an interesting family reunion?

The fact that so many famous Americans are related is not surprising when you consider that 82 percent of all Americans have at least one ancestral line which is of English, Welsh, Scottish, or Irish background.

- More than 100,000 people are known to be descendants of England's Edward III, and through Edward are related to many royal lines of the Middle Ages.

- In ancient China and Japan, ancestors became personal family gods. Deceased forebears were believed to oversee and influence events on earth, and had responsibility for continuing filial piety and harmony among the living.
- Islamic countries consider the study of ancestry important because their prophet, Mohammed, taught them to "Learn of your genealogical tree as much as is needed for the practice of active love toward blood relatives."
- In certain African tribes, an ancestor's status in the hereafter depends upon the memory of the living. Every family makes a concentrated effort to think highly of the dead so that the quality of afterlife for the deceased will be enhanced. The expression "Don't speak ill of the dead" may have originated here.
- In Ireland, the Irish Genealogical Association plays host to family reunions every summer. The lure of the Emerald Isle is enough to bring hundreds of aunts, uncles, and cousins to Ireland.

Family history

Prior to the twelfth century, Western ancestral history was oral, and belonged to the realm of story-tellers and balladeers. When family history needed to be written, clergymen took over the job. Many a flawed character was transformed into a person of saintly proportions with the flick of a pen. We might say their acts were cleaned up. Too many people know about the dastardly deeds of a relative? No problem—simply saw off the limb from which he figuratively or literally hung. A lot of wayward kinfolk have been lopped off during careful pruning of the family tree.

Modern technology has made genealogical search faster, but the excitement remains. Locating ancestors entails the skill of Sherlock Holmes and the patience of Job. Just as you locate one elusive relative, reference to another pops up and the chase is on again.

One of the major difficulties in tracing relatives very far back in time is that the number of potential ancestors increases dramatically with each preceding generation. Everyone has 2 parents, 4 grandparents, 8 great-grandparents, 16 double greats, 32 triple greats, and 64 quadruple greats, with like doubling in every preceding generation. That would mean that in the year 400, you would need to locate some 18.5 quintillion ancestors . . . if it worked that way. That's more than the number of people who ever lived. How can that be? Common ancestors, that's how. If we could accurately trace our family tree as far back as the beginning of time, we would see how we are all interrelated. Somewhere along the way, cousins had to marry cousins whether they knew they were related or not.

Immediate sources

The old axiom about the apple never falling far from the tree isn't going to be of much help, because family apples can be found as close as next door, or clear around the world.

Start with yourself. Your first clue to your ancestry is your name. (If your family has maintained a documented family tree for generations, this advice may seem unnecessary, but for beginners it will prove invaluable.)

Write your family name at the top of the page. Next, list possible variations. Have any relatives changed their name? Is your name frequently mispronounced? Books on **onomastics** provide information on the origin, meaning, and evolution of names.

There are several different formats (placement of names, dates, interesting anecdotes) you may use. To discover the methods preferred by genealogists, and to choose those you are most comfortable with, a trip to the library is in order. A good guide is Val D. Greenwood's *The Researcher's Guide to American Genealogy,* published by the Genealogical Publishing Company.

Tracing your family's history always begins with you and your immediate family members. Elderly relatives are a wonderful source of information. Peruse old photographs, family Bibles, scrapbooks, or other records. In faded tintypes or dog-eared photos you will see reflected images of yourself. You may discover that a son who doesn't resemble anyone in the family looks exactly like a great-granduncle, or you can tell the daughter who wondered about her red hair that among family souvenirs is a strand of coppery-red hair that provided the same lovely glow to a great-great-grandmother.

A terrific source of family history is a relative by marriage. The interesting stories are often suppressed by *blood* kin, but in-laws never forget. Some of my father's greatest stories were those he told about my mother's side of the family. Story-telling sessions often ended with my father in the doghouse.

Many libraries offer seminars on the use of videotape to document family history.

Write letters to distant relatives (figuratively distant as well as physically). Provide a list of questions for them, and include a self-addressed stamped envelope to encourage their co-operation. When you receive your replies, don't forget a thank-you note.

More distant sources

When you have exhausted the more intimate family sources, contact Active kin, friends, former neighbors, and religious institutions.

Vital statistics include birth, death, marriage, and naturalization records. By 1920 all states had begun registration of births and deaths. Prior to that time statistics were recorded in a rather haphazard manner, or not at all. As late as 1898 only seventeen states required compilation of vital statistics.

Visit the county Register of Deeds office to study contracts, deeds, leases, maps, and mortgages. Surrogate, Probate, or Orphans Courts are the place to examine copies of wills, adoption papers, changes of name, and petitions for guardianship.

State archives have higher court papers, census enumerations, and older vital records. Federal records contain census, land, court, immigration, and military information.

The Church of Jesus Christ of Latter-day Saints has the largest collection of genealogical information in the world. Contact the Family History Library (The Church of Jesus Christ of Latter-day Saints), Genealogical Department, Dept. P, 35 N. West Temple Street, Salt Lake City, Utah 84150-0001.

The National Archives sponsors an annual genealogical seminar. Classes are taught by experts in the fields of census records, legal records, military history, colonial handwriting, cartography, migration patterns, oral genealogy, and so forth.

There are patriotic, lineage, and ethnic societies to aid you. In addition to well-known groups like the Daughters (Sons) of the American Revolution (D.A.R. and S.A.R.), and United Daughters of the Confederacy, there are the Spanish War Veterans, Sons of Confederate Veterans, Descendants of the Signers of the Declaration of Independence, the Ladies of the Grand Army of the Republic (for female descendants of Union soldiers), and the Aztec Club of 1847 (for descendants of servicemen of the Mexican War).

Cemeteries are sources of names, dates, and relationships.

School and college records provide excellent sources of information because applications usually list family members and dates. Since the 1920s, grammar schools have taken yearly pictures of the children and usually preserve a master photograph and a roster of names.

If all of this seems a bit much, you can hire someone to do the tedious work for you. For a list of persons certified to do genealogical research, contact the Board of Certification of Genealogists, P.O. Box 19165, Washington, D.C. 20036.

Holidays and special family events bring together several generations. Why not make a record of these wonderful times? Childhood memories surface, older relatives are available to reminisce, and children can add their impressions.

There are several computer software programs available. I like the Genealogical Management System for Home Computers (Personal Ancestral File) from the Church of Jesus Christ of Latter-day Saints, Genealogical Department, at 50 E. North Temple Street, Salt Lake City, Utah 84150. At $35.00 the package is a bargain.

Why research?

Does it seem strange to look back in order to look forward? It shouldn't. We are who we are because of who they were. Without understanding the feelings and faults, values and virtues, joys and jobs, and sorrows and successes of your ancestors, all you have left is a series of "begats."

In Alex Haley's *Roots* there are a few sentences near the end of the book which summed up for me everything there is to say about ancestors. Mr. Haley relates a conversation between his mother and his grandmother:

> *It was the talk, I knew, that always had generated my only memories of any open friction between Mama and Grandma. Grandma would get on that subject [her ancestors] sometimes . . . and Mama always before long would abruptly snap something like, "Oh, Maw, I wish youd stop all that old-timey slavery stuff, it's entirely embarrassing!" Grandma would snap right back, "If you don't care who and where you come from, well, I does!"*

Alex Haley is eternally grateful that his grandmother cared enough to remember, and he has spent many hours and travelled thousands of miles to connect with "kinfolk."

10 • Kinship and the Future

When I was just a little girl
I asked my mother, "What lies ahead?
Will there be rainbows, day after day?"
Here's what my mother said:
"Que sera sera (Whatever will be will be)".
                                    Popular song from the 1950s

The Population Institute estimates that sometime in 1986 the five billionth person was born as a "sobering symbol" of world population growth.

Whoever the new person was, or whenever the child was born, at the twilight of his lifetime his concept of "kinship" may be, in many ways, vastly different from ours. Lumped in with the scientific and technological advances that can be expected will be changes within the family itself.

Sociologists are seriously concerned whether the'family will even exist in its present form. The customs surrounding courtship, marriage, birth, kinship, and death which we currently hold dear may languish in the graveyards of the dim, distant past. Might our grandchildren be so sophisticated and unsentimental that neither custom, nor superstition, nor tradition will embellish the special events in their lives?

In most societies, great ceremony attends birth, coming of age, marriage, and death. Humans have always managed to combine the ridiculous with the sublime when it comes to these rites of passage. Some customs are necessary, some are funny, some are sad, and some are just plain silly, but in each

103

generation we embrace our idiosyncratic beliefs with the zeal
of an itinerant tent revivalist.

Families in the future

In the future, people will have many choices in terms of the
family life they elect to pursue. They may choose the traditional
family, which used to be the only acceptable game in town, or
they may choose to remain single.

Should they decide not to marry, they may opt to have
children either with a willing partner, with the assistance of a
surrogate mother, or using donated sperm. According to the
Census Bureau, nearly one out of four women who had a child
in 1990 wasn't married. Twenty-five percent of those children
were born into families where the mother and father hadn't
married but did live together.

Others might choose to live in what the Census Bureau
calls "Other Households." Since the bureau's definition of a
family requires a blood relationship, this category includes
homosexual couples, unmarried heterosexual couples, and
roommates of all ages who simply live together for financial or
emotional support.

There will be more effort by gay couples to force legal
acceptance of their lifestyles, which would accord them
traditional inheritance rights and health benefits generally
reserved for traditional married couples.

One thing is certain: the traditional American nuclear
family—two parents and their children living together under
one roof—is rapidly disappearing. Blended families where one
or both spouses bring children to the marriage are the fastest
growing type of family. Nearly one-third of all Americans now
live in blended (step-family) situations.

Regardless of these changes and the difficulties inherent in
the family's evolution, most Americans value the family and its
demise is highly unlikely.

Kinship, who needs it?

When all is said and done, it doesn't really matter how kinship is figured. There are no clear-cut definitions which must be adhered to. Whether your society calculates degrees of cousin-hood, and another refuses to accept the existence of such a relationship; whether you say great-aunt, and I say grandaunt; whether kinship is calculated bilaterally (affiliated with relatives both maternal and paternal), or unilaterally (connected mainly with either father or mother); whether descent is traced mat-rilineally (through the mother) or patrilineally (through the father), or even ambilineally (the individual is given a choice of which heritage to choose); whether one family traces their genealogical background for centuries and another can't locate a single grandparent... none of it matters beyond the fact that kinship is a basic organizing principle. Kinship is the unifying ingredient of family life in all societies.

Kinship places us in a network of status and resources, rights and responsibilities, plus giving and receiving of assistance in times of need, along with rejoicing in times of happiness and tears in times of grief. Even if any and all kinship functions can be taken over by institutions,, kinship remains important.

What really matters about kinship are the emotions, the overlapping relationships, the interaction between generations (the loving as well as the feuding), and the knowledge of our heritage. These are the reasons why people research their ancestors, diagram family trees, and hold family reunions.

Kinship, who needs it? Indeed, we all do.

Epilogue

O what a tangled web we weave!

When I wrote to my cousin, Moody Smith, about my intention to write a book regarding kinship and degrees of relationship, he answered by telling me a story that could have happened in the South of not so long ago, when families were started at such an early age that it was difficult for a stranger to distinguish parent from child.

Moody told me the tale of Ferd, a widower, and his only son, Roscoe, who lived with him. Ferd dug ginseng roots, raised a little garden patch, and collected commodity cheese and dried milk. Jim-Bob, a neighbor two hills over, had a thriving business and Roscoe worked for him. Roscoe didn't report his wages because his job mostly consisted of carrying hundred-pound sacks of sugar through the woods.

The only women for several miles around belonged to Jim-Bob: his wife Roxie, and their almost-ripe daughter, Trixie. Each day at lunch time Roxie and Trixie would come down from the house and bring a platter of hot baloney sandwiches for Jim-Bob and Roscoe to eat.

Roscoe knew the business pretty well by the time the still blew up and took Jim-Bob with it. Roscoe quickly wooed and won Roxie, garnering for himself a business, a family, and hot baloney sandwiches three times a day.

Ferd started hanging around, and at night the four of them would sit around, play cards, and tell ghost stories. On the day that Trixie finished turning ripe, Ferd was right there to pick her—the two of them hopped in Jim-Bob's old pickup truck, drove over the state line and got married. Both women conceived shortly thereafter. In due time, Roxie gave birth to Bubba, and Trixie had Buster.

Roscoe was very happy. The only fly in the ointment was that Ferd seemed content to just sit back and let Roscoe support him, all the while eating Roxie's hot baloney sandwiches. Remembering the way Jim-Bob had gone, Roscoe determined to make a will—and that's when his life changed. He tried not to think about his situation, for each time he did, he began drinking his profits.

"How in the world can I provide for my daddy if I cut my shiftless son-in-law out of my will? My daddy is married to my wife's daughter, therefore he is my son-in-law. My stepdaughter, Trixie, is my stepmother. She is Roxie's daughter, but because she is my daddy's wife, she's also Roxie's mother-in-law. Trixie is Ferd's wife, but because she's my daughter, she is also Ferd's granddaughter. Little Bubba is my son, but because he is my stepmother's brother, he is also my uncle—I'm my own son's nephew.

Little Buster is my wife's grandson, so he is my grandson, too, but because he is my daddy's boy, he is also my brother. Because he is my brother, he is Bubba's uncle—so my grandson is my son's uncle. Bubba is Trixie's brother, so he is Buster's uncle. Both of them little boys are each other's uncle. That makes Trixie Bubba's sister, grandmother, and grandaunt."

Roscoe's thoughts continued, "Ferd is my daddy, and Bubba is my son, so Ferd is Bubba's granddaddy; Ferd is married to Bubba's sister, so he is Bubba's brother-in-law. Trixie is Ferd's wife, so she is Bubba's grandmother. That makes Roxie Bubba's great-grandmother, as well as his momma. If that little boy's mother is also his great-grandmother, then I have to be his great-grandfather. And because I am my son's great-grandfather, that makes me my own grandpa. Can I really be my own grandpa?"

Roscoe scratched his head, ruminated a little, and went on, "Let me look at this from another direction. Buster is my brother and Roxie is his grandmother, so I am my brother's granddaddy. Ferd is my daddy, so that makes him Buster's great-granddaddy, too. And if my daddy is also my great-granddaddy, than I just have to be my own grandpa. Yep, that is what I am, my own grandpa."

Roscoe made a quick decision to quit thinking about the mess he had going, and he dumped his problem in the lap of a local lawyer.

There may be glaring holes in Roscoe's reasoning, but it's highly possible that at some time in the jurisprudential past, some poor judge became entangled in an intestate estate squabble (one where there was no will) in which the squabblers were interrelated in a can of worms similar to Roscoe's.

After a night of fitful sleep, the judge awoke knowing what he had to do. Early that day, he hied himself to the state legislature—where, with no thought or knowledge of concomitant regressive genes, he prevailed upon his cronies to pass laws to keep close kin from getting so close that he and his colleagues might go crazy whenever it came time to sort out the closeness.

Such is the stuff of which kinship is made.

Bibliography and Reference List

This bibliography is by no means a complete record of all the works and sources I have consulted. It does, however, indicate the range of reading upon which I have formed many of my ideas.

Aginsky, Bernard Willard. *Kinship Systems and the Forms of Marriage* The American Anthropological Association, 1995

Ashley, Leonard R. N. *What's in a Name?* Genealogical Publishing Company, 1989

Ashley, Paul P. *You and Your Will.* McGraw-Hill, 1977

Baselt, Fonda D. *The Sunny Side of Genealogy.* Genealogical Publishing Company, 1988

Bright, Joseph E. *To Will or Not to Will.* Dennis & Company, 1937

Byrne, Julia Clara. *Curiosities of the Search Room.* Chapman & Hall Ltd., 1880

Considine, Millie and Ruth Pool. *Wills—A Dead Giveaway.* Doubleday & Company, 1974

Dawkins, Richard. *The Selfish Gene.* Oxford University Press, 1976

Family and Kinship in Chinese Society. Stanford University Press, 1970

Fox, Robin. *Kinship and Marriage: An Anthropological Perspective.* Penguin, 1974

—*Reproduction and Succession: Studies in Anthropology, Law, and Society.* Transaction Publishers, 1993

Frazer, J. G. *Totemism and Exogamy.* Macmillan, 1910

Galeener-Moore, Laverne. *Collecting Dead Relatives.* Genealogical Publishing Company, 1987

Gillis, John. *For Better, For Worse: British Marriages, 1600 to the Present.* Oxford University Press, 1985

Goody, Jack. *The Development of Family and Marriage in Europe.* Cambridge University Press, 1983

Gormley, Myra Vanderpool. *Family Diseases: Are You at Risk?* Genealogical Publishing Company, 1989

Greenwood, Val D. *Researcher's Guide to American Genealogy.* Second edition. Genealogical Publishing Company, 1990

Holding on to the Land and the Lord: Kinship, Ritual, Land, Tenure, and Social Policy in the Rural South. University of Georgia Press, 1982

Homans, George Casper. *Marriage, Authority, and Final Causes: A Study of Unilateral Cross-Cousin Marriage.* Free Press, 1955

Hughes, James Pennethorne. *How You Got Your Name.* Phoenix House, 1959

Kohler, Josef. *On the Prehistory of Marriage: Totemism, Group Marriage, Mother Right.* University of Chicago Press, 1975

Lerner, Gerda. *The Creation of Patriarchy.* Oxford University Press, 1986

Reed, Evelyn. *Woman's Evolution from Matriarchal Clan to Patriarchal Family.* Pathfinder Press, 1975

Schneider, David Murray. *American Kinship: A Cultural Account.* Prentice-Hall, 1968

Skalka, Lois Martin. *Tracing, Charting and Writing Your Family History.* Pilot Books, 1975

Stannard, Una. *Married Women Versus Husbands' Names.* Germain Books, 1973

Shoumatoff, Alex. *The Mountain of Names: A History of the Human Family.* Simon and Schuster, 1985

Technologies of Procreation: Kinship in the Age of Assisted Conception. Manchester University Press, 1993

Wake, Charles Staniland. *The Development of Marriage and Kinship.* University of Chicago Press, 1967

Westin, Jeane Eddy. *Finding Your Roots.* Ballantine Books, 1977

Woodward, Kenneth, and Arthur Kornhaber. *Grandparents/ Grandchildren: The Vital Connection.* Transaction Books, 1985

Yorburg, Betty. *The Changing Family.* Columbia University Press, 1973

Glossary

A

Adopt: to take into one's family the child of another, with the rights, privileges, and duties of one's own child and heir

Agnate: persons related through male descent

Affinity: relationship created by marriage

Ancestor: a progenitor; a forefather

Annulment of marriage: a judicial pronouncement that a marriage was void from the beginning

Antecedent: a relative who precedes one in the line of descent

Ante nuptial: prior to the marriage

Artificial insemination: introduction of semen into the uterus by means other than intercourse

Ascent: order of genealogical succession

Aunt: a sister of one's father or mother

B

Banns: notice of a proposed marriage, proclaimed in a church or other place required by law, in order that anyone with valid reasons may object

Bastard: a child born out of wedlock

Bigamy: the act of marrying one person while legally married to another

Biological parent: a person who provides the sperm or ovum to produce a child

Birthright: any right, privilege, or possession to which a person is entitled by birth

Bride: a woman about to be married; a recently married woman

Bridegroom: a man about to be married; a recently married man

Brother: a male person having the same parents as another person

Brother-in-law: the brother of one's spouse

Byname: a name in addition to the first; a secondary name

C

Canon law system: one of several systems of legal rules by which inheritances are regulated

Cater cousin: a first cousin

Christian name: a personal first name selected for a child born into a Christian home

Clan: a social unit smaller than a tribe, larger than a family, and claiming descent from a common ancestor

Cognant relative: a person related to another on the mother's side

Collateral line: a line of descent that is oblique rather than straight; collaterals descend from a common antecedent but can neither ascend to nor descend from other collateral relatives

Collateral relatives: persons related by blood but not in a direct line

Common law marriage: a private arrangement between a man and a woman without a wedding ceremony or observance of legal requirements

Concubine: a woman who cohabits with a man without being married to him

Consanguinity: the quality or state of being related by blood

Cousins: relatives who share a common grandparent; the relationship of children of siblings

Cousins-german: first cousins

Cousins-removed: persons who are related as cousins, but belong to different kinship generations

Cross first cousins: the children of a brother and a sister

Curtsey: a husband's legal share in his wife's estate (statutory share)

D

DNA: deoxyribonucleic acid associated with the transmission of genetic information

Daughter: a female offspring

Daughter-in-law: the wife of one's son

Decedent: a dead person

Degree: a step in a direct line of descent or of ascent to a common ancestor

Degree of relationship system: one of several legal systems used to determine heirs in intestate succession

Descend: to come down or spring from a stock or source

Descendant: a person descended from specific ancestors

Descent: the established connection between an individual and his progenitors

Double first cousins: children born when siblings of one family marry siblings of another family; cousins who share all lineal and collateral relatives

Dower: a wife's legal portion of her husband's estate (statutory share)

Dowry: the property a woman brings to her husband

E

Endogamy: breeding within the basic social group as required by custom or law

Exogamy: breeding outside the basic social group as required by custom or law

Extended family: a family group which includes near relatives and in which collateral lines are kept fairly distinct

F

Family: parents and their children; persons related by blood or marriage

Family name: the surname that identifies an individual with his family

Family of affinity: the family of one's spouse; the in-laws

Family of orientation: the family into which one is born

Family of procreation: the family created when one marries

Family tree: a schematic description of genealogical relationships

Father: a man who has begotten a child

Father-in-law: the male parent of one's spouse

Fictive kin: persons who are considered to be family even though they are not related by blood

First cousins: the relationship of children born to siblings; children who share a common grandparent

Forensic genealogy: research of a pedigree for legal purposes

Foster: nurture that is not available from one's own parents

Foundling: a child deserted by his or her parents

Fraternal twins: two children born as a pair at one birth, but conceived from separate ovum

G

Gene: one of the elements of the germ plasm serving as specific transmitters of heredity characteristics

Genealogy: an account or history of the descent of a person, family, or group from an ancestor

German: a full or whole degree of consanguinity

Given name: the personal name bestowed upon a person at birth

Godchild: a child who is sponsored at baptism by a person who promises to oversee the religious development of that child

Godfather: a male who sponsors another at a baptism and promises to oversee the religious development of that person

Godmother: a female who sponsors another at a baptism and promises to oversee the religious development of that person

Grandaunt: an aunt of one's father or mother

Grandchild: a child of a one's son or daughter

Granddaughter: a daughter of one's son or daughter

Grandfather: the father of one's mother or father

Grandmother: the mother of one's father or mother

Grandnephew: a grandson of one's sibling

Grandniece: a granddaughter of one's sibling

Grandson: a son of one's son or daughter

Granduncle: the uncle of one's mother or father

H

Half relative: any familial relationship in which the degree of kinship is not whole

Heir: a person who is legally entitled to inherit

Hypergamy: social superiority of the female

I

Identical twins: two children born as a pair from the same mother, and having been conceived from one ovum

Idiot-savant: a person whose mental functions are severely limited except for one exceptional talent

Illegitimate: one who is born of parents who are not married to each other

Immediate descent: a direct line of descent from parent to child

In loco parentis: in the place of a parent

Incest: sexual intercourse between closely related individuals

In vitro fertilization: fertilization of an ovum outside the living body, as in a test tube

Intestate: the legal designation for one who dies without making a will

K

Kinsman: a man related by blood or sometimes by marriage
Kinswoman: a woman related by blood or sometimes by marriage
Kin: a group of persons of common ancestry
Kindred: a group of individuals related by blood
Kinship: the biological relationship shared with others; family relationship
Kissing kin: certain collateral relatives so distantly related that marriage is not restricted by law
Kosher: food ritually prepared for use according to Jewish law

L

Legitimize: to give a bastard the legal status of a legitimate child
Line: a succession of ancestors or descendants of an individual, family, race
Lineage: descent from a common progenitor
Lineal: consisting of or being in a direct male or female line of ancestry

M

Maiden name: the birth surname of a woman
Marriage: the state of being united to a person of the opposite sex as husband and wife
Maternal: behaving in a motherly way
Maternal line: related through the mother's side
Matriarch: a woman who rules over the family, usually to the exclusion of males in her family
Matriarchy: a system of social organization in which descent is traced primarily through the female line
Matrilineal: tracing descent through the mother
Mediate descent: when there is another ancestor intervening between two related people, such as from grandfather to grandson
Miscegenation: marriage between persons of different races
Mitochondrial DNA: a peculiarity in cell structure which only females pass through their daughters
Mother: a female who gives birth to a child; a female parent

N

Name: a word or sound by which an individual or class of individuals is regularly known or designated

Nephew: a male child of one's brother or sister

Niece: a female child of one's brother or sister

Next-of-kin: a person in the nearest degree of relationship by blood, marriage, or court decision

Nuptial: of or relating to marriage or the marriage ceremony

O

Orphan: a person who has lost one or both parents, especially one who has lost a father Ovum (Latin, egg): the female reproductive cell of animals

P

Parallel first cousins: the relationship of children born to brothers

Parent: one who begets or brings forth offspring, or stands in the place of biological parents

Parentelic system: a system used in determining which heirs receive a share in intestate cases

Paternal: related through one's father

Paternal line: ascent or descent traced through the father's lineage

Paternity: the state of being a father

Patriarchal family: a family ruled by the father in both domestic and religious functions

Patrilineal: lineage traced through the father and organized on the basis of male descent and inheritance

Patronymic: a name derived from that of a paternal ancestor, usually by adding a special prefix or suffix

Pedigree: a register recording lines of ancestors; alludes to the form in which family tree charts were drawn in the Middle Ages, from the French pied de grue (crane's foot)

Per capita: a method of dividing an intestate estate by which equal shares are given to each of several persons who stand in equal degree to the decedent

Per stirpes: the system whereby a person takes the share to which their deceased ancestor would have been entitled

Phratry: a social tribal subdivision based on kinship

Polyandry: a marriage in which a female has two or more legal husbands at the same time

Polygamy: a marriage in which a spouse of either sex may possess several legal mates at the same time

Polygyny: a marriage in which a man has two or more legal wives at the same time

Primogeniture, rule of: an inheritance system under English law in which the eldest son or the eldest male in the next degree of consanguinity succeeds to an estate to the exclusion of females and younger males of equal degree

Progenitor: an ancestor in a direct line

Progeny: offspring; children

R

Relative: a person connected with another by blood or affinity

Removed: belonging to generations separated by a given degree of lineal consanguinity; used in law only with respect to cousins

S

Second cousins: the relationship of children born to first cousins; persons who share a common great-grandparent

Sib: related by blood; brother or sister

Siblings: two or more persons who have the same parents

Son: a male offspring

Spouse: one's lawfully wedded mate

Statutory share: a term representing the husband's share of his wife's estate (curtsey) and the wife's share in her husband's estate (dower)

Stepfather: a man who is not one's biological father, but is the husband of one's mother

Stepmother: a woman who is not one's biological mother, but is the wife of one's father

Surname: the name shared by members of a family

Surrogate: a person who acts in the place of another

T

Tangential relatives: not closely related

Teknonymy: the custom of naming the parent after the child

Testate: to die without making a legally valid will

Testator: someone who has made a legally valid will before death
Testatrix: a woman who has made a legally valid will before death
Tribe: a social group comprising numerous families, clans, or
generations together with dependents

U
Uniform Probate Code: a legal method of determining inheritance
Ultimogeniture, rule of: a system of inheritance by which the youngest
son succeeds to an estate

V
Vital statistics: data that record significant events and dates in human
life, such as births, deaths, and marriages

W
Wedding: the marriage ceremony and its attendant festivities
Will: a legal document detailing the distribution of one's property
after one's death

Z
Zygote: a fertilized ovum

Index

A
Acquired Immune Deficiency
    Syndrome, AIDS 13
Adoption 12, 25, 52, 53-55, 88
    adult 55
    annulments 13, 55
    National Committee 54
    Uniform Adoption Act 54
Affinity, family of 25, 46
Affines (in-laws) 12, 46, 83
Agnatic 5
Artificial insemination 54, 89
Ascent 27, 28, 32
    ancestor 25, 27, 28, 32, 36
    collateral 27, 28
    lineal 27
Ashley, Leonard R.N. 75
Aunt 28,33-35,36,38,45
    grand 36

B
Bigamy 10
Boleyn, Anne x
Bush, George, President 97
Brother (see sibling)

C
Carter, Jimmy, President 97
Children 25, 50-55, 73, 83
    foster 51
    foundling 51
    illegitimate 52
    legitimate 80
Church of Jesus Christ of Latter-
    day Saints (see Mormon)

Clan 4, 26
Cognate 2, 3, 5
Cohabitation (live-in) 17-18, 62
Collateral 28
Consanguinity
    definition of 33
    chart of 34
Courts
    Orphan's, Probate, Surrogate
    100
Cousins 12, 28, 38-45, 56
    cater 38
    cross 43, 44
    double 43, 44
    first 12, 13
    german 38
    parallel (ortho) 43, 44
    quarter 38
    removed 12, 39, 40
Cousins, how to calculate 40
Cryopreservation 57, 58
Curtsey 79

D
DNA, mitochondrial 3
Daughters of the American
    Revolution, National Society
    of (DAR) 1, 53, 101
Descendant 27-28, 32
    collateral 27, 28
    lineal 27
Descent 5, 27, 28
    agnatic 5
    cognant 5
    immediate 27

lineal 27,
  mediate 27
Divorce 16, 17, 47, 64
Dower 79

E
Edward VIII, King 9, 97
Elizabeth II, Queen of England
  relationship diagram 41
Endogamy 4
Estrous 2
Exogamy 4

F
Family, defined 7, 49
  history 98
Family, types of 2, 18, 25, 26,
  29, 31-47, 53,104-105
  financial support of 56
Family law 49, 50, 56-58, 62, 63
Foster, defined 51
Foundling, defined 51

G
Genealogy 97-101
  horizontal 97
  matrilineal 3
  parallel 97
  patrilineal 3
Genealogists, Board of
  Certification 101
Generations 32, 35, 36
Genetic 1, 85-89
Grands 36, 45
Grandparents, rights of 58-62
Greats 36, 45
Greenwood, Val D. 99

H
Haley, Alex 102
Henry VIII, King x

I
Incest, civil ix, 4, 5, 12, 19, 21

In-laws (see affines)
Intestate estate 81
  parentelic system 81
  relationship system 81
  Uniform Probate Code 81, 82
In vitro fertilization 89

K
Keane, Noel 90
Kinship, chart of consanguinity
  34
Kinship, types of 2, 3, 5, 25,
  27-29, 32, 44, 83,105

L
Legitime 80
Legitimate 7, 52

M
Marriage, 5, 7-24
  legal requirements 10, 11,
  19-24
  premarital agreements 14, 50
  prohibitions 10-13
  rights 15-16
  types of 8, 9
Matrilineal 2
Mohammed, the prophet 51
Monogamy 5
Mormon (Church of Jesus Christ
  of Latter-day Saints)
  10, 80, 86, 101
Mother 45, 46, 56
  surrogate 54, 90

N
Names 71-75
  changes 74
  children 73
  married women, surnames
  of 72
Napoleon 1, of France x
Nixon, Richard, President 97
Nephew 28,35
Niece 28,35

O

Orientation, family of 31-47
Outbreeding (*see* Exogamy)
Orphans 51
Ortho (*see* Cousins, parallel)

P

Palimony 18, 50
Parent 25, 36, 38, 43, 45, 50, 54
Paterfamilias xi
Paternal 2, 32
Patriarchy 3-5
Pedigree 1
Phratry 4
Polyandry 11
Polygamy 10
Polygyny 10
Primogeniture, rule of 78

R

Relationship, degree of 29, 33, 37
    diagram 37
    removes 39

S

Sept 4
Sibling 4, 12, 27, 28, 31, 32, 33, 36, 38, 46
Simpson, Wallis Warfield 9
Smith, Moody 107
Sister (*see* Sibling)
Statistics vital 63-69, 100
Surrogacy 89, 90

T

Toulouse-Lautrec, Henry Marie Raymond 87
Thatcher, Margaret 78
Tribe 4, 26
Twins 31, 32

U

Ultimogeniture, rule of 78
Uniform Probate Code 81
Uncle 28, 33-35, 36, 38, 45

V

Victor, Richard S. 59
Vital statistics 63-69, 100

W

Wilson, Allan C. 3
Wills 77-83
    canon law system 81
    degree of relationship system 81-82
    holographic 81
    oral 80
    parentelic system 81-82
    statutory share (*see* Dower and Curtsey)
    Uniform Probate Code 81-82
Wynette, Tammy 16

Same-Sex Marriage

The Heart has its reasons which the mind knows nothing about.

Blaise Pascal

If William Shakespeare were alive and well and writing today, he might paraphrase his famous quote something like this: "To marry or not to marry, that is the question," and he would have to add the disclaimer "… and who may I legally marry, Romeo or Juliet?" That is the question he might be compelled to ask if he were living in the twenty-first century in the United States of America. Such a question would have been unheard of in Shakespeare's day. It isn't as if human beings 400 years ago were not subject to the same desires of the heart as we are—they were, but it was the sort of thing you might have been burned at the stake for even considering.

Frequently we must look to the past in order to understand the present. Since recorded history, religion has been a determining factor in the belief that marriage is between a man and a woman. Opposite-sex marriage is a tradition in all major religions including Christianity, Buddhism, Islam, and Judaism.

Religious beliefs account for some of the negativity regarding gays (a term used to describe both homosexual men and women) wishing to enter into a legally recognized marriage. Proponents of same-sex marriage say past rejection and persecution of the gay community was abhorrent, and everyone must now put aside such archaic teaching. They say monogamous consenting adults should be able to do as they wish, and as long as no one gets hurt, it is nobody's business but their own.

Opponents of same-sex marriage say they have gone about as far as they are willing to go on homosexual rights. They say they have accepted that people are different and will reluctantly tolerate such behavior as long as their noses are not rubbed in it. However, they say they do not have to like it, and they draw the line at what they view as surrendering the last bastion of the straight world: marriage.

History

In a 1996 Internet article called "Lesbian and Gay Marriage through History and Culture," Paul Halsall examined the history of homosexual alliances and gave examples that indicated past societies had many different interpretations of the word "marriage":

- one man and many woman (polygyny)—Islam, ancient Israel
- one man with a chief wife and subordinate wives and/ or concubine—China
- one woman and many men (polyandry—Tibet
- one man where the man was usually an adult about 30 and one woman about 15 years old—Classical Athens, Renaissance Italy
- one man and one woman approximately the same age in an arranged marriage—some Orthodox Jews, many Indian and Chinese societies
- one man and one woman because they love each other—the modern norm, and often traced back to the Protestant Reformation.

Mr. Halsall says what these marriages appear to have in common is cohabitation, recognition, rules of conduct, ceremonials, and the amount of time participants spend together. Legal recognition is not required in all instances; for example, in modern Scotland it is still possible to be married by "habit and repute." In several U.S. states this is known as "common-law" marriage, and is legal and binding upon the participants if they hold themselves out to the community as husband and wife. When a common-law marriage ends, it must be dissolved by a legal divorce. Common-law marriages were once recognized in most states, but many states no longer recognize them. The federal government does not recognize common-law marriages as far as federal benefits are concerned.

While not referred to as legal marriages, committed homosexual relationships have been discovered as far back as Egypt's King Niuserre of the Fifth Dynasty in the tomb of Niankhkhnum and Khnumhotep. It was obvious the tomb had been constructed so the two men could co-habit in the afterlife. In life, both men shared the same occupational title: Overseer of the Manicurists in the Palace of the King. (See "United For Eternity," *KMT: A Modern Journal of Ancient Egypt*, vol.4, no. 3, 1993.)

Since King Niuserre's reign there have been numerous historical examples of homosexual unions, yet none of them can be factually confirmed as legal or binding. In fact, some accounts have been viewed as satirical writings by ancient scholars, attempting to convey wit and humor. It is reported that Rome's Emperor Nero went through a wedding ceremony with a freedman (a former slave). Nero dressed as a bride, and on the "wedding night" he imitated a female's reaction. He had earlier gone through a wedding ceremony with a young boy whom he dressed as a bride and treated as his wife for a time. It is doubtful that either situation was ever considered legal, but more likely an example of Nero's penchant for play-acting.

We do not have to go so far back in history to find a culture that allows "woman marriage." Among the Nuer in Sudan a woman can marry another woman, thereby becoming the "father" of the children of the "wife." The word "pater" is the title given to the woman who takes the "husband" role. "Genitor" is the word for the male friend or neighbor who is used to impregnate the wife of the pater. To make the marriage official, the pater must pay a bridewealth (compensation from the husband's family to the bride's family). The pater takes on all the social roles of a man and, if wealthy, she is able to take as many wives as she wants.

In some historical social situations, the familial term most often given to same-sex relationships was "brother" for males and "sister" for females, which designated a fictive kinship. Today, we often address a close unrelated male or female by the honorific "uncle" or "aunt" without any sexual inference.

Marriage

The names and types of opposite-sex marriages and relationships, homosexual unions, partnerships, and cohabitations throughout the long history of a multitude of religions and secular cultures are much too lengthy to enumerate in this chapter, but individuals may do further research through their local library or the Internet. Two good Internet sources are: "Lesbian and Gay Marriage through History and Culture," by Paul Halsall **(gay. bible.org)**; and "Cultural Anthropology/Marriage, Reproduction and Kinship" **(wikibooks.org)**.

In a nod to future social and legal acceptance, all major English dictionaries have revised their definition of the word *marriage*. They drop gender specifications, supplement them with secondary gender-neutral definitions, or explicitly recognize same-sex unions. The *Oxford English Dictionary* has recognized same-sex marriage since the year 2000.

In modern American and Western European society, the traditionally acceptable marriage of a man and a woman is monogamous, and is several thousand years old in both religious and secular society. Even in countries allowing plural marriage, it is still one man with multiple women (polygyny) or, less often, one woman with several men (polyandry).

So here we are in the twenty-first century with the federal government firmly against same-sex marriage by the Defense of Marriage Act (DOMA), which was enacted by the 104th

Congress and signed into law by President William Jefferson Clinton. The bill amends the U.S. Code to make explicit what has been de facto practice for over 200 years: marriage is the legal union of one man and one woman as husband and wife, and a spouse is a husband or wife of the opposite sex. Under the law, no state may be required to recognize a same-sex relationship considered legal marriage in another state. The law does not yet recognize same-sex marriage for any federal purposes.

DOMA was passed in anticipation that Hawaii and perhaps other states would soon legalize same-sex marriage. Opponents feared, and proponents hoped, that all other states would then be required to recognize such marriages under the Full Faith and Credit Clause (Article IV, Section 1) of the United States Constitution.

The main provision of the act reserves powers to the states by declaring that no state, territory, or possession of the United States, or Indian tribe, is obligated to respect a relationship between persons of the same sex who were legally married in other jurisdictions. In other words, the basic purpose of the act is intended to release states from any obligation to recognize marriages of same-sex couples coming from other states.

Connecticut, Iowa, Massachusetts, New Hampshire, New York, Vermont, Washington, Washington, D.C., the Coquille Indian Tribe of Oregon, and the Suquamish Indian Tribe in the state of Washington choose to ignore DOMA and allow same gender couples to marry. In another instance of how quickly laws can change, the State of Maryland recently passed a bill to accept same-sex marriages as legal, and became the eighth state to do so.

DOMA also addresses bi-national same-sex couples, and prevents them from legally living in the United States as a married couple. Because of this, an American citizen who is a member of a same-sex marriage cannot confer his partner with permanent residence by virtue of their union. However, if one member of the same-sex couple is threatened with deportation because the legal resident cannot sponsor the partner for a green card (which grants permission to remain and work within the United States), humanitarian parole is granted on a case-by-case basis at the Department of Homeland Security Secretary's discretion.

However, prior to 1996, the federal government did not define marriage. Any marriage valid in a state was recognized as valid by the federal government. Legally married couples are entitled to a multitude of rights and protections conferred to U.S. citizens including Social Security benefits, veterans' benefits, tax deductions, and healthcare coverage, though under DOMA, this now only applies to opposite-sex couples.

Some opponents of same-sex marriage seem to feel that while a horse may be called a pig, that doesn't make it a pig, and you cannot get bacon from it. Proponents might respond to such sentiment by saying they do not want to call a horse a pig, but they do want the bacon (i.e., federal and state benefits extended to opposite-sex marriages).

Appeals are pending both for and against the Defense of Marriage Act, so careful and constant review of state and federal law is essential. The rulings come so fast and furious that on a given day two same-sex persons might have permission to marry and the next day have that permission withdrawn. In California, same-sex couples who obtained licenses and married prior to Proposition 8 in 2008 (by which voters eliminated the right of same-sex couples to marry) are accepted as legally married. Those couples who waited were temporarily out of luck, as same-sex marriages were put on hold pending further appeal.

Proposition 8 was subsequently overturned in federal court, with a stay on the decision supposed to be lifted on August 18, 2010 allowing same-sex unions to resume, but on August 16, 2010 the stay was extended by a higher court. However, just recently, the proposal was once again reversed, giving hope to couples still wishing to marry in California. Opponents of same-sex marriage vow to mount further protests.

Some mainstream professional associations assert that scientific evidence contradicts the stereotype-based arguments advanced to support DOMA, and make claims that federal government discrimination between same-sex and opposite-sex married couples harms those families and their children.

Legislation called the Respect for Marriage Act was introduced in Congress to repeal DOMA, but was not supported because others felt the law could be overturned more quickly through lawsuits filed by the Gay and Lesbian Alliance Against Defamation (GLAAD.) The constitutionality of DOMA is also under attack, but early challenges in federal courts have failed, while others have succeeded but are still under appeal. Legalization of same-sex marriage has so far been achieved by court rulings and legislative action, but not yet through voter referendums.

While the legal benefits of marriage are numerous, same-sex couples would find themselves faced with the same financial constraints as opposite-sex couples, including, as one example, the marriage penalty in the federal tax code. Also, while social services providers usually do not count one partner's assets toward the income means test for welfare and disability assistance for the other partner, a legally married couple's joint assets are normally used in calculating whether a married individual qualifies for assistance.

Family

In a May 2008 research brief by Joshua Baker, published by the Institute for Marriage and Public Policy (iMAPP), the link between marriage and procreation and survival of the human race is examined. Mr. Baker says, "Marriage is a socially recognized unit best situated for raising children within the legitimacy and stability of a state-sanctioned relationship. Courts have upheld that encouraging the raising of children in homes consisting of a married mother and father is a legitimate state interest."

Opposite-sex supporters say that men and women may marry regardless of whether the couple can produce children—older couples, infertile couples, or those choosing not to have children may marry, but homosexual couples may not, no matter how committed they are to each other.

Today, however, many parents and extended family members must come to terms with the relationships their children or other kindred have with their same-sex life partners. Some people are being asked to discard their beliefs and embrace marriage of two people of the same gender. Will they be able to welcome these partners with open arms, or will they slam the door in their faces? If the door is closed, parents run the risk of alienating their off-spring and severing family ties. Alienation, rather than acceptance, is often the response.

What about grandchildren? Through marriage and procreation a family ensures the continuation of the next generation. Legal heirs are produced only within a valid marriage. Modern methods of conception (in vitro, surrogacy, adoption) make it possible for same-sex partners to have children, but these methods bring other problems: legality, social acceptance, inheritance, and other dynamics come into play. Prospective grandparents also worry about other problems their grandchildren may have to deal with when they are raised in a non-traditional home.

Recent studies of children in same-sex relationships suggest the possibility these children may have difficulty in social adaptation and understanding gender roles when entering society unless the couple carefully inform the children about their unique situation. Any perceived difference in youthful social situations is often cause for bullying. Children with two parents of the same gender are immediately recognized as different. Schools are becoming more sensitive to bullying, but punishing the offender does not erase the pain suffered by the person being bullied. It takes a strong child to stand up to social pressure regarding the life situation in which they find themselves. If gender specific terms like "mom" and "dad" are used in same-sex parental situations, will this confuse a child whose friends call their female parent "Mom" and the male parent "Dad"?

It would be interesting to see a study concerning whether children of two male partners do better socially than children of two females. Society, rightly or wrongly, might view families headed by female same-sex couples as weak. Does the sex of the child make any difference in how a child is treated in social situations? Some research shows that pubescent girls are the worst of all bullies because they tend to use more hidden aggression and carry the aggression much further than boys (see *Odd Girl Out,* by Rachel Simmons (New York: Harcourt, 2002).

Then, again, other studies have shown that children of opposite-sex parents have problems adjusting to the demands of society, and these adjustments are no harder or easier than children parented by same-sex couples. It must be borne in mind that surveys are often conducted using methods to justify the beliefs and desires of the researching entity, so you have to be careful when relying upon results. Many an argument has been won with the nebulous statement "Studies have shown …" without knowing whether the study was biased or not.

An analysis of 2000 census data conducted by the Urban Institute and the Human Rights Campaign, published in 2001, concludes:

1. Same-sex couples live in 99.3 percent of all counties nationwide.
2. There are an estimated 3.1 million people living together in same-sex relationships in the United States.
3. Fifteen percent of these same-sex couples live in rural settings.
4. One out of three lesbian couples is raising children. One out of five gay male couples is raising children.
5. Between 1 million and 9 million children are being raised by lesbian, gay, and bisexual parents in the United States today.
6. At least one same-sex couple is raising children in 96 percent of all counties nationwide.
7. The highest percentages of same-sex couples raising children live in the South.
8. Nearly one in four same-sex couples includes a partner 55 years old or older.
9. More than one in 10 same-sex couples includes a partner 65 years or older, and nearly one in 10

same-sex couples is composed of two people 65 or older.

10. The states with the highest number of same-sex senior couples are also the most popular for straight senior couples: California, New York, and Florida.

Religion

Mainstream religion tends to be conservative. Most major religious organizations condemn any type of homosexual behavior, and while the winds of change may have begun to blow, Evangelical religious organizations quote Biblical scripture to validate their opinion that homosexuality is a sin and an abomination to God.

Prominent church leaders have varying opinions about gay marriage. Rick Warren, author and pastor of Saddleback Church in California, said in an interview, "Nowhere in the Constitution can you find the 'right' to claim any loving relationship identical to marriage." He also said, "I'm opposed to having a brother and sister being together and calling that marriage. I'm opposed to an older guy marrying a child and calling that marriage. I'm opposed to one guy having multiple wives and calling that marriage." When asked if he considered those examples to be equal to allowing gays to marry, he said he did, and added "... Christians, Buddhists, Muslims, and Jews ... historically [believe] marriage is between a man and a woman."

Joel Osteen, author and pastor of Lakewood Church in Houston, Texas, seemed to hedge his bets when asked on a television talk show about gay marriage. He said he wouldn't officiate at a same-sex marriage, but he would attend the wedding ceremony if the partners were good friends of his. He went on to say that according to scripture, homosexuality is wrong.

Bishop (now Cardinal) Timothy Dolan of New York said New York's law alters "radically and forever humanity's historic understanding of marriage." In a public statement, he said "... this definition cannot change, though we realize that our beliefs about the nature of marriage will continue to be ridiculed, and that some will even now attempt to enact government sanctions against churches and religious organizations that preach these timeless truths." Pope Benedict XVI has recently stated the Roman Catholic Church is opposed to gender neutral marriage.

Politics

In the political arena, former House Speaker, presidential candidate, and thrice married Newt Gingrich called same-sex marriage a "temporary aberration" that will eventually disappear because it defies convention. Mr. Gingrich's half-sister is a lesbian in a same-sex marriage who says her brother is out of touch with the times.

In 1996, President Clinton claimed he was opposed to gay marriage, but later opined he personally supports same-sex marriage but "doesn't believe it's a federal question." President Obama's views have also undergone a revision over time, and he claims his "views [on same-sex marriage] are evolving." He opposed same-sex marriage early in his career but has since backed off that position. He has also stated he believes DOMA is unconstitutional and will soon be repealed.

Secretary of State Hillary Clinton, seeking to raise awareness in other countries regarding a less punitive stance toward gays, says the United States may use threats of withholding foreign aid to promote gay rights worldwide. American gay rights advocates are taking a leadership role, but obviously the United States cannot change laws in other countries, stop abuse, or change minds. The current president of Iran claims there are no homosexuals in that country, so they don't even consider it a problem worth addressing.

Influence of Celebrity

In the cultural arena, the influence of gay celebrities has had a major impact. Celebrity activists have begun to push to the mainstream same-sex relationships, and the more popular the celebrity, the more accepting the fans become.

Film, stage, and television personalities openly voice their opinions about their sexual preferences. Famous people who live a gay life style continue to make their life choices known to the public.

The list of celebrities in same-sex relationships is long, but most prominent at the moment are actress, talk-show host and comedian Rosie O'Donnell; situation comedy performer and talk-show host Ellen DeGeneres (Ellen and her partner were married in California prior to the court battle over Proposition 8, so their marriage is considered legal); singer Melissa Etheridge; and financial guru Suze Orman (who was married in South Africa to her female companion). They make no secret of their private lives.

Great Britain's Sir Elton John, musician and song-writer, is married to his long-term partner and they have a child conceived with the help of a surrogate.

Political commentators such as Glenn Beck and Rush Limbaugh are among the most conservative talk-show hosts, and yet their views on same-sex marriage are very different. Beck says he doesn't believe gay marriage is a threat to the United States. Limbaugh says, "... this is about tearing apart an institution."

Genealogy

Genealogy is the study of tracing the lineage of a particular family. Kinship is based on the relatedness to people through descent, sharing, or marriage which has been traditionally between one man and one woman.

Genealogists are asking themselves if and how legalization of same-sex marriage will affect family trees. They were already reeling from the effects on research of children conceived by surrogacy, sperm and egg donors, and in vitro fertilization, and now must cope with single mothers, single fathers, significant others, domestic partnerships, civil unions, and same-sex married couples.

Some researchers differentiate between genealogy and family history, and limit genealogy to tracing kinship (bloodlines), while others follow both kinship and family history. A family history approach seems better able to incorporate the aforementioned methods of procreation now available.

Bloodlines, thanks to advances in genetics, have become easier to trace using the three types of DNA: mitochondrial (direct female); the Y-chromosome (direct male); and the autosomal DNA, which is found in the 22 non-specific chromosomes (autosomes) inherited from both parents and can identify relatives from any branch of the family. These methods are particularly useful when children born outside the normal method of conception seek to discover their bloodlines and relations. Of course, DNA is not helpful if an ancestor is several hundred years removed and there is no DNA material to examine. DNA analysis can determine if a forebear came from a particular area of the world, but it works best when DNA is available from a recent common ancestor. However, as individual test results are collected in databases, future matches should be more readily available.

Until the advent of computer programs and databases, genealogists had to spend hours in courthouses and libraries, and many more hours interviewing living relatives. Information was usually recorded on 3X5 index cards and then transferred onto charts. The Internet has certainly changed the way in which genealogists work, but they are still on the prowl for that elusive ancestor. It has been said that genealogists must have the zeal of an itinerant preacher and the stamina of a detective. Regardless of the obstacles, however, genealogists are a resourceful lot, and will surely develop methods to deal with complicated family histories.

No doubt we will continue for some time to struggle with the idea of same-sex relationships in regard to civil unions, domestic partnerships, and legal marriage. Change comes slowly and is often attended by pain and suffering for all involved, but somehow we always end up exactly where we are supposed to be.

Same-Sex Marriage Laws in the United States by State

The following is a condensed version of current legal and political actions taken by individual states as of this printing. Because laws and public acts are constantly changing, depending on the ebb and flow of information, partisan attitudes, and special interest groups, it is advisable that you consult legal experts in your state of residence.

Alabama: A marriage between individuals of the same sex is invalid. No marriage license or recognition, no other relationship or its recognition from other jurisdictions for same-sex couples.

Alaska: Legal marriage is between a man and a woman. A marriage entered into by persons of the same sex, either under common law or under statute, even if recognized by another state or foreign jurisdiction, is void in this state, and contractual rights granted by virtue of the marriage, including its termination, are unenforceable.

Arizona: Only a union of one man and one woman shall be valid or recognized as a marriage. A marriage between persons of the same sex is void and prohibited. No marriage license or recognition, no other relationship or its recognition from other jurisdictions for same-sex couples.

Arkansas: Marriage consists only of the union of one man and one woman. Marriages between persons of the same sex are prohibited. However, an employer may extend benefits to persons who are domestic partners of its employees.

California: Currently only marriage between a man and a woman is valid in this state, as defined by Proposition 8, a constitutional amendment. This amendment is currently under siege by same-sex couples and civil rights groups.

Colorado: Only a union of one man and one woman shall be valid or recognized as a marriage. No marriage license or recognition of same-sex marriage; however, a few rights are granted to domestic partners through a designated beneficiary agreement.

Connecticut: This state's marriage laws are gender neutral, stating that marriage between two persons is valid. Same-sex marriages from other jurisdictions are recognized.

Delaware: A marriage is prohibited and void between persons of the same gender. No marriage license or recognition, no other relationship or its recognition from other jurisdictions for same-sex couples.

District of Columbia: In 2009 the Religious Freedom and Civil Marriage Equality Amendment Act became law. Same-sex marriages are now performed in the District of Columbia, which recognizes same-sex marriages performed in a state or country where they are legal.

Florida: This state limits marriage to opposite-sex couples. "Inasmuch as marriage is the legal union of one man and one woman, no other legal union that is treated as marriage or the substantial equivalent thereof shall be valid or recognized." No marriage license or recognition, no other relationship or its recognition from other jurisdictions for same-sex couples.

Georgia: This state recognizes as marriage only the union of man and woman. No marriage license or recognition, no other relationship or its recognition from other jurisdictions for same-sex couples.

Hawaii: A valid marriage contract shall be only between a man and a woman. Reciprocal Beneficiaries (the existing form of domestic partnership in Hawaii) extends certain rights and benefits to couples composed of two individuals who are legally prohibited from marrying under state law. No marriage license or recognition from other jurisdictions for same-sex couples.

Idaho: A marriage between a man and a woman is the only domestic legal union valid or recognized. No marriage license or recognition, no other relationship or its recognition from other jurisdictions for same-sex couples.

Illinois: Current law recognizes only a marriage between a man and a woman. A marriage between two individuals of the same sex is contrary to the public policy of this state. No marriage license or recognition, no other relationship or its recognition from other jurisdictions for same-sex couples.

Indiana: Only a female may marry a male. A marriage between persons of the same gender is void in Indiana even if the marriage is lawful in the place where it is solemnized.

Iowa: It is a legal opinion that same-sex couples may marry in this state; however, this ruling is under appeal. According to the Associated Press, out-of-state marriages of same-sex couples are recognized in Iowa.

Kansas: Marriage is to be considered as a civil contract between two parties who are of opposite sex. No marriage license or recognition, no other relationship or its recognition from other jurisdictions for same-sex couples.

Kentucky: As used and recognized in the law of the Commonwealth, marriage is between one man and one woman. Marriage is prohibited and void between members of the same sex. Same-sex marriage in another jurisdiction is void and unenforceable.

Louisiana: Marriage shall consist only of the union of one man and one woman. No official or court of the state shall recognize any marriage contracted in any other jurisdiction which is not the union of one man and one woman.

Maine: Same-sex marriage in this state is currently unrecognized. Domestic partnerships are recognized.

Maryland: A bill was recently passed allowing same-sex marriage, but challenges are forthcoming. Until this is resolved, only a marriage between a man and a woman is valid. However, certain/few rights are granted to domestic partners through unregistered cohabitation.

Massachusetts: In 2004, the state began to issue marriage licenses to same-sex couples. No explicit prohibition on recognition from other jurisdictions for same-sex couples, but no other relationship or its recognition from other jurisdictions for same-sex couples.

Michigan: A marriage contracted between individuals of the same sex is invalid. The state constitution states the union of one man and one woman in marriage shall be the only agreement recognized as a marriage. No marriage license or recognition, no other relationship or its recognition from other jurisdictions for same-sex couples.

Minnesota: Marriage between persons of the same sex is prohibited. No marriage license or recognition, no other relationship or its recognition from other jurisdictions for same-sex couples.

Mississippi: Marriage may take place and may be valid only between a man and a woman. Any marriage between persons of the same gender is prohibited and null and void from the beginning. No marriage license or recognition, no other relationship or its recognition from other jurisdictions for same-sex couples.

Missouri: It is the public policy of this state to recognize marriage only between a man and a woman. Any purported marriage not between a man and a woman is invalid. No marriage license or recognition, no other relationship or its recognition from other jurisdictions for same-sex couples.

Montana: A marriage between persons of the same sex is prohibited. No marriage license or recognition, no other relationship or its recognition from other jurisdictions for same-sex couples.

Nebraska: Only a marriage between a man and a woman shall be valid or recognized. The uniting of two persons of the same sex in a civil union, domestic partnership, or other similar same-sex relationship shall not be valid or recognized. No marriage license or recognition, no other relationship or its recognition from other jurisdictions for same sex couples.

Nevada: Only a marriage between a male and female person shall be recognized. No marriage license and no marriage recognition from other jurisdictions for same-sex couples. However, domestic partnership arrangements are legally available.

New Hampshire: Marriage is the legally recognized union of two people. Any person who otherwise meets the eligibility requirements may marry any other eligible person regardless of gender. Every marriage legally contracted outside the state which would not be prohibited under New Hampshire law shall be recognized as valid in this state. Civil unions are also valid.

New Jersey: Under this state's constitution, committed same-sex couples must be afforded on equal terms the same rights and benefits enjoyed by opposite-sex couples under the civil marriage statutes. The name to be given the statutory scheme that gives full rights and benefits to same-sex couples, whether marriage or some other term, is a matter left to the democratic process. No explicit texts on same-sex marriage. Civil unions are recognized within the state and are acceptable from other jurisdictions.

New Mexico: No marriage license, but no explicit prohibition on recognition from other jurisdictions for same-sex couples.

New York: A bill permitting same-sex marriage was passed by the state legislature in 2011.

North Carolina: A valid and sufficient marriage is created by the consent of a male and female person who may lawfully marry and take each other as husband and wife. Marriage between persons of the same gender is not valid. No marriage license or recognition, no other relationship or its recognition from other jurisdictions for same-sex couples.

North Dakota: Marriage consists only of the legal union between a man and a woman. No other domestic union, however denominated, may be recognized as a marriage or given the same or substantially equivalent legal effect. No marriage license or recognition, no other relationship or its recognition from other jurisdictions for same-sex couples.

Ohio: A marriage may only be entered into by one man and one woman. Any marriage between persons of the same sex is against the public policy. No marriage license or recognition, no other relationship or its recognition from other jurisdictions for same-sex couples.

Oklahoma: A marriage in this state shall consist only of the union of one man and one woman. A marriage between persons of the same gender performed in another state shall not be recognized as valid.

Oregon: Only a marriage between one man and one woman shall be valid or legally recognized as a marriage. Although no marriage license or recognition for same-sex couples, domestic partnerships have been recognized since 2008.

Pennsylvania: Marriage is between one man and one woman. A marriage between persons of the same sex which was entered into in another or foreign jurisdiction, even if valid where entered into, shall be void in this Commonwealth.

Puerto Rico: In 1998, Puerto Rico ratified the Defense of Marriage Act (DOMA). No marriage license or recognition, no other relationship or its recognition from other jurisdictions for same-sex couples.

Rhode Island: In 2011 this state legalized civil unions for same-sex couples. Same-sex marriages and other relationships from other jurisdictions are recognized as civil unions.

South Carolina: A marriage between one man and one woman is the only lawful domestic union that is valid or recognized in this state. No marriage license or recognition, no other relationship or its recognition from other jurisdictions for same-sex couples.

South Dakota: Only marriage between a man and a woman shall be valid or recognized. The uniting of two or more persons in a civil union, domestic partnership, or other quasi-marital relationship shall not be valid or recognized in this state. No marriage license or recognition, no other relationship or its recognition from other jurisdictions for same-sex couples.

Tennessee: The legal union in matrimony of one man and one woman is the only recognized marriage in this state. No marriage license or recognition, no other relationship or its recognition from other jurisdictions for same-sex couples.

Texas: Marriage shall consist only of the union of one man and one woman. No marriage license or recognition, no other relationship or its recognition from other jurisdictions for same-sex couples; however, two people of the same gender can marry if one of them is transgendered based on Littleton v. Prange which defines that a person's sex is determined by birth.

Utah: Marriage consists only of the legal union between a man and a woman. Same-sex marriage is prohibited. No marriage license or recognition, no other relationship or its recognition from other jurisdictions for same-sex couples.

Vermont: Marriage is the legally recognized union of any two adult persons (not gender specific). Other relationships from other jurisdictions for same-sex couples are recognized as marriage.

Virginia: Only a union between one man and one woman may be recognized as a valid marriage. Marriage between persons of the same sex is prohibited. No marriage license or recognition, no other relationship or its recognition from other jurisdictions for same-sex couples.

Washington: Marriage is a civil contract between a male and a female. Marriage is prohibited when the parties are persons of the same sex. No marriage license or recognition, no other relationship or its recognition from other jurisdictions for same-sex couples. However, a bill has been passed to accept gay marriage, but the bill is under appeal.

West Virginia: No marriage license or recognition, no other relationship or its recognition from other jurisdictions for same-sex couples.

Wisconsin: Only a marriage between one man and one woman shall be valid or recognized as a marriage. Marriage licenses are not issued to same-sex couples; however, certain limited rights in a domestic partnership are legally provided for and are recognized from other jurisdictions for same-sex couples.

Wyoming: Marriage is a civil contract between a male and a female person. No marriage license or recognition, no other relationship or its recognition from other jurisdictions for same-sex couples.

CPSIA information can be obtained at www.ICGtesting.com
Printed in the USA
BVOW030857210513

321260BV00007B/33/P